The Library of Pastoral Care

TITLES ALREADY PUBLISHED

Sick Call: A Book on the Pastoral Care of the Physically Ill
Kenneth Child

Caring for the Elderly
H. P. Steer

The Pastoral Care of the Dying
Norman Autton

The Pastoral Care of the Bereaved
Norman Autton

Casework and Pastoral Care
Jean Heywood

Marriage Preparation
Martin Parsons

IN PREPARATION

The Principles of Pastoral Care
R. S. Lee

The Pastoral Care of the Emotionally Distressed
Chad Varah

Marriage Counselling
Kenneth Preston

The Pastoral Care of Children
Eric Mathieson

The Pastoral Care of Adolescents
Michael Hare Duke

The Priest's Work in Hospital
Norman Autton

Retreats
W. R. Derry (editor)

Other volumes are planned

Library of Pastoral Care

MARRIAGE PREPARATION

BY THE SAME AUTHOR AND PUBLISHED BY
HODDER & STOUGHTON LTD

Your Marriage
The Holy Communion
The Ordinal
A Christian's Guide to Growing Old

Marriage Preparation

MARTIN PARSONS

LONDON

S·P·C·K

1967

First published in 1967
by S.P.C.K.
Holy Trinity Church
Marylebone Road
London N.W.1

Made and printed in Great Britain by
William Clowes and Sons, Limited
London and Beccles

TO
EMILY
a succourer of many,
and of myself also

Contents

Acknowledgements

Thanks are due to the following for permission to quote from copyright sources:

Hodder and Stoughton Ltd: *The Practice of Evangelism*, by B. Green.

Longmans, Green and Co. Ltd and David McKay Company Inc.: *Background to Marriage*, by Anne Proctor.

Lutterworth Press and Oxford University Press (New York): *Vocabulary of the Bible*, by J. J. von Allmen.

S.C.M. Press: *Secular Despair and Christian Faith*, by A. Vidler.

An Introduction to the Theology of the New Testament, by Alan Richardson: copyright © 1958 S.C.M. Press Ltd, reprinted with the permission of Harper & Row, Publishers Inc., New York.

Foreword by the Bishop of Chelmsford

The great majority of marriages in this country are stable and happy. The statistics of divorce do not necessarily mean that marriage is held in less regard than heretofore. I believe that the great majority of young people today have a high ideal of what marriage ought to be and that anything that helps them at a crucial moment in their lives is gladly received.

I commend to the clergy and others this handbook on Marriage Preparation. The Church still has a great opportunity in this sphere. There is abundant evidence to show that almost all clergy look upon their duty in this matter as one of great pastoral importance.

Success in this field yields results that accrue more and more as the years go by. For marriage preparation really begins long before marriage. Thus a couple fully prepared in every sense are already laying firm foundations for their children, who, by their upbringing in an atmosphere of family stability, discipline, and contentment, will be fitted for the day when they themselves will prepare for marriage.

Mr Parsons writes out of a long experience as a parish priest. When, as is here described, theory and practice come together, the advice given and the experiences shared must be valuable to all who have the task of guiding men and women in the duties and joys of married life.

1 June 1967   JOHN CHELMSFORD
                    A Clerical Adviser to
                    The National Marriage Guidance Council

Preface

In writing about the work of preparing people for marriage I have tried to cover all the ground. Inevitably therefore I have written some things which to all but the complete novice will appear obvious and hardly worth saying. I seek the indulgence of the reader who is experienced in these things, if indeed any such should bother to read the book. It is not meant for them. I have all along been thinking of those who are just beginning. They will develop their own techniques, and certainly, I hope, improve on mine. But perhaps what I have tried to say will give some idea of the importance of the subject and the almost immeasurable opportunities it presents of fulfilling one's ministry.

I am no specialist, but have had to give time to marriage preparation from a programme as full as that of many other clergymen. It has meant that some aspects of the ministry have been neglected, for one cannot do everything. Yet I have no regrets about this. I regard this work as supremely important.

Not only am I not a specialist, I am not an expert either. I am sure that any parish priest can do what I have tried to do, and many can do it much better. Somebody had to write down the kind of things that have got to be considered, and for some reason I am that one. I alone am responsible for what is here written, for the simple reason that no-one ever taught me how to do these things. Perhaps I can save a few of my younger brethren from some of the snags we are bound to meet.

I am grateful to all who have helped me with encouragement and comment, and especially to the Reverend Stanley

Birtwell for reading the manuscript and making useful suggestions.

Oxford   MARTIN PARSONS
11 August, 1966

1

The Opportunity

"It is to be hoped that the days when the parties saw the parish clerk or verger to put in the banns, and met the parish priest for the first time at the wedding, are now over." So wrote Charles Forder twenty years ago in his monumental book on Pastoralia, *The Parish Priest at Work*.[1] This wishful remark was not in vain: nowadays we should no more think of marrying a couple in church without some kind of preparation than we would present candidates for Confirmation who had not been instructed. This certainly was not always the case. Even today we cannot be sure that the preparation is adequate.

There may be good reasons for this. One is that in a large parish, where at certain times of the year there can be ten or more weddings on a single Saturday, there simply is not the time to give each couple the individual attention which is desirable. Another is that the clergyman is not fully trained in this side of his work. To say that he ought to have been given detailed instruction in his Theological College is to betray ignorance of the overcrowded programme of training and of the limitations inherent in the classroom teaching of pastoral techniques. A third reason for the inadequacy of some marriage preparation is a failure on the part of the clergyman to recognize the urgency of the task and the unparalleled opportunity it gives him to exercise his ministry.

Canon Hugh Warner, who did as much as any man to bring home to the clergy the supreme importance of this work, used to place it third in his list of priorities in consider-

[1] S.P.C.K. 2nd edition (revised) 1959.

ing the claims on a minister's time (this did not include the personal devotional life which everyone knows must come before all else). First he put the conduct of worship and all that goes with it by way of preparation. Second came the care of the sick, which in a sense is an extension of the first to those who are unable to attend church. And third was the preparation of couples for marriage.

He was surely right in putting it high on the list. Here are people coming to their parish priest and saying, "We want your help." So much of our work seems to consist in trying to create a sense of need for what we have to offer. Even when we visit the sick we are not always sure that we are wanted. But when a couple comes to the Vicarage door to arrange about the wedding they show that they want what we have to give. They may indeed be thinking of little more than a white wedding, with music and bells, and some kind of "blessing", the nature of which they would not find it easy to describe. But it is something that they come to the Minister of God's Word and Sacraments and ask him for what he has to give.

However vague may be their thoughts about the sanctity of marriage, we have to remember that they are open to what we have to say as at few other times in life. This is not a case of taking advantage of people who are on the crest of an emotional wave in order to force our religion on them. Rather is it an opportunity to help them to understand the real nature of love and the divine institution of marriage, and so to lead them to God, who is the author and giver of all good things.

Holy Matrimony is one of the Occasional Offices, which does not mean that it seldom takes place, but that when it does take place it marks a great occasion. Like Baptism and Burial it happens—for most people—only once. All the hopes and fears which a young couple entertain as they stand before this tremendous step make them peculiarly ready for the guidance which we can give them at such a time. In preparing hundreds of couples for marriage I have met with varying degrees of responsiveness. But hardly ever have I sensed any feeling of resentment, and in innumerable cases there has been obvious gratitude. Perhaps those who might resent our efforts to help them are more likely to go to the Register Office than to the Vicarage.

Most people will agree that it is a good thing that civil marriage is available for those who do not want a church wedding. A division of opinion occurs when it comes to deciding whether or not to welcome all who apply for a marriage service in church. Are we going to limit the privilege of being married with the Church's blessing to those who are practising church people? Or are we going to accept anyone who is baptized and expresses a desire for a Christian marriage service? There is no doubt that the latter is the historic and legal practice in the Church of England, but there are those who believe that in the present missionary situation in this country it is no longer realistic.[1]

We can fully sympathize with the desire to confine the use of Christian services to Christian people. The difficulty is in judging who is a Christian and who is not. If we demand that a person be a regular communicant, we have to define what we mean by "regular". Someone who comes once a year on Easter Day is regular. It seems better to take the more traditional view of giving our ministry to those who ask for it. In the first instance they may only be asking for a ceremony which has more dignity and colour than a Register Office wedding. Yet this gives us the opportunity of teaching them why a marriage service in church is "different", as they so often express it.

And do we really know that this is not what they are seeking when they come to us? Even apparently "hard-boiled" young people stand in awe before the mystery of marriage and the solemn responsibilities of their wedding vows. There

[1] It has to be remembered that we are not legally allowed to turn people away, with certain exceptions which are discussed in chapter 5.

is often a deep sense of inadequacy which *we* know is an inarticulate expression of the need for God. They may be looking for advice, or guidance, or reassurance, or just the friendship of someone who really cares about their deepest happiness. Through this we may be able to lead them to a truly Christian understanding of love and marriage, and to commitment to Christ.

While therefore we shall always try to safeguard the service of Holy Matrimony from becoming a merely social occasion, it is doubtful if we shall achieve this by turning people away. There will be disappointments, just as there are among those we prepare for Confirmation. But there will also be great joys, and if the results are not always seen immediately, at least the seed has been sown.

2
The Purpose

Controversy rages today about the function of the Church in modern society. To state the matter in crude terms, there are those who hold that the Church's mission is to win people to itself, and there are those who react violently from this notion and say that the Church is here to serve the world rather than to convert it. Surely there is no compromise to either principle if we say that both are true. No one who takes the New Testament seriously can deny that the first duty of a Christian is to witness to Christ and by every means in his power to pass on his faith to others. In practice it is generally found that the larger part of this evangelistic witness is through the quality of loving service which Christians show to all who need help. If it is indeed *loving* service, it will be disinterested; the spontaneous outflow of the love of Christ, offered freely, irrespective of any response it may gain. Yet loving service will not stop short of sharing the very best treasure that we have, the only ultimate answer to all life's questings, Jesus Christ himself.

The bearing of this on the priest's work of preparing people for marriage is obvious. Ultimately his aim is to bring the couple to that commitment to faith in Christ, and life in his Church, which is the only true basis to a successful and happy marriage. But he must at all costs avoid giving the impression that all that he does for the couple is no more than a means to an end. He is concerned for the well-being of the whole man, and must genuinely believe that everything about the wedding, even down to the details of arrangements which have little to do with the religious service, is really important. He is there to try to be helpful, to offer his service in every way possible to those who have come to ask for it. He will give help at every level, quite irrespective of whether or not there is any obvious response to his more direct evangelistic approach. Anything like ecclesiastical scalp-hunting will be readily detected, and confidence will be lost, and rightly so. Yet all the time the true pastor knows that the greatest help he can offer is to lead the couple a stage further along, or often only towards, the path of Christian discipleship.

What then is the purpose of marriage preparation? First, to ensure that everything will go without a hitch on the wedding day. This is the point of immediate contact. The couple are totally inexperienced in arranging a wedding. We have the "know-how", and can do a lot to help them. Though we may have taken hundreds of weddings, we shall never forget that for each couple it is an absolutely unique event. The priest must be as attentive to detail in each case as if it were his own daughter who was being married.

While we are genuinely interested in every part of the day's proceedings, our particular concern is for the details of the service. When we come to consider the technique of the interviews we shall see that going through the service in the Prayer Book provides ample opportunity for discussing numerous aspects of marriage. But we must not overlook the simple purpose of ensuring that the bride and bridegroom know what to do and what to say at each point, and understand what they are doing and the reasons for it. This is all part of a ministry directed to the total needs of those we serve. A well-conducted service, for which everybody concerned has been properly prepared, is a good start. It will not of itself ensure a happy marriage any more than, thank God, a slovenly and ill-prepared service need mean that the marriage itself will not be supremely happy; but the outward details do matter, and do have an effect.

Secondly, the purpose of marriage preparation is to show the couple that a happy marriage is the will of God. It is called Holy Matrimony not simply because it is solemnized in church but because it is in itself a holy institution, a part of God's loving plan for the highest of his creatures. The Church has not always encouraged this belief. There have been times when it has fallen into the heresy of regarding celibacy as a higher state, and marriage as a concession to human weakness. It is extraordinary how hard this view dies, not so much within the Church itself but in the minds of those on the fringe who think this is what the Church teaches. Without falling into the opposite error of deifying sex, we need to show it as the good gift of God "who endows us richly with all things to enjoy" (1 Tim. 6.17).

It is something of a revelation to many couples to realize that the achievement of a successful and happy physical relationship within marriage is as much a part of God's will for them as that they should say their prayers or read their Bible together. Yet this is certainly the case. Any help we can give them in coming to understand the spiritual significance of sex is pastoral care of the highest order. Marriage of course has other purposes besides the hallowing of "the natural instincts and affections implanted by God", and we shall be ready to help with advice on every aspect, but we must recognize as basic the one thing which distinguishes marriage from any other close friendship.

A third purpose in marriage preparation is to set clearly before the couple the privileges of the gospel and the claims of our Lord upon their life. If they see that we are interested in them as people rather than as potential pew-fodder, they will be prepared to listen to what we have to say as part of our convictions about the ingredients of a true marriage. We should not be in the Ministry at all if we did not believe that man's supreme need is "that they know thee the only true God, and Jesus Christ whom thou hast sent" (John 17.3).

This is in fact the relationship which affects all other relationships, and not least the marriage bond.

So in the course of our preparation we shall make it clear that we all need what only God can give: forgiveness, reconciliation, newness of life, fellowship in the Body of Christ. The way in which we put it will vary for each couple, for they are all at different stages. Our efforts may often be only a kind of pre-evangelism and we may have to be satisfied with having put the case, and having perhaps awakened some faint desire for the things of God. On the other hand we may be preparing a couple who are both eager Christians, ready to discuss fully how their faith is to be worked out within the new setting of their marriage and their home.

What makes this work so exciting is the infinite variety of people that we see. We can never reduce the art of marriage preparation to a stereotype routine. Each couple is different and must be treated accordingly, with great respect for their individuality. They do not come to be lectured, but to find a friend who is ready to offer them help of any kind. This is the fourth purpose of marriage preparation, to establish a pastoral relationship.

This will certainly entail a sharing of concerns on a wide variety of subjects. Guidance may be needed about parents or parents-in-law, hire purchase or life insurance, or a thousand and one matters to do with the home, the job, or the wedding reception. Nothing is trivial to *us* which is of importance to *them*. We are building a bridge. We may wait for years before we see any crossing of the bridge. Sometimes another priest in another parish will reap where we have sown. There may often appear to be no fruit at all. But no caring is ever wasted. The number of candidates for Confirmation, or professions of conversion, is not the only criterion of success. Our Lord cleansed ten lepers simply because he had compassion on them, and though he grieved over the nine, he did not grudge them the healing they had received. So we must give the very best we have, whatever we may see or not see in return.

Unfortunately many of those whom we prepare for marriage will be moving away to another parish. It is to be hoped that the care we take in setting up a good relationship will be a help to some other priest who takes up the contact. We may have helped to convince a couple that the clergy, as a class, are approachable, friendly, and helpful. In commending a couple to their new vicar it will be found valuable to make use of the S.P.C.K. form, with its counterfoil to be kept for reference.

3

Who Can Do It?

Granted the importance of the work of preparing people for marriage, is it something which every priest should be expected to do? Is this not rather something for the expert who, with special training as well as natural aptitude, will bring professional efficiency to an admittedly difficult task? There is a good deal of sense in such a question. Experiments in Group and Team Ministries are encouraging the development of specialization in many directions. Why not, therefore, a Marriage Preparation Specialist in every Rural Deanery? Would there not then be some certainty that the work would be well done?

Attractive as the suggestion may appear, there would seem to be a strong case for the opposite idea. One of the complaints made about specialization in medicine is that the old doctor-patient relationship is not so personal as it used to be. This is something which must not happen to the pastor-people relationship. Even in these days of shorter incumbencies, the average vicar can look forward to staying in a parish till some of his Confirmation candidates are old enough to marry. Having prepared them for Confirmation and watched over them in the intervening years, is he to send them to a comparative stranger, however expert, to be prepared for so big a step? He will probably feel that he has done some of the preparation already, in the course of his regular ministerial work, and will not want to give away a supreme pastoral opportunity.

It must be admitted that some of the clergy are very much

better at this work than others. The same is true about preaching, and every other branch of our ministry. But the advantages of an all-round pastoral care are great, and far outweigh any lack of skill in one direction or another. So every parish priest should consider it a part of his personal ministry to prepare people for marriage, not to delegate it to others even though they may be better qualified. This does not preclude the calling in of experts to deal with some particular problem: this should be done in any branch of pastoral work. In a later chapter we shall discuss co-operation between the clergy and the Marriage Guidance Council.

Some might feel that an unmarried clergyman is at a disadvantage in this kind of work. This need not be the case. Dr Vidler once said in justification of his preaching on the subject of marriage:

> ... while married people who discuss this subject have certain plain advantages derived from their actual experience, yet they normally have complete experience of only one particular marriage to go by, and this is liable certainly to influence and also very likely to distort their judgment about marriage in general, since one marriage differs from another both in its glory and in its torment. Moreover, this is an area of human life where in some ways the onlooker sees most of the game; anyhow, it is a game of which no one who moves at all in society can help seeing a great deal.[1]

There might well be some limit set on the age at which an unmarried priest should begin the work of marriage preparation. This should probably be related both to actual age and to years of experience in the ministry. A priest ordained at the minimum age might be asked to delay starting until he is twenty-six, by which time he will have had three years of experience in a parish, and such training as his incumbent has been able to arrange for him. Some older men come into the ministry with an experience of dealing with people which qualifies them to begin at once. Basically there is nothing in

[1] *Secular Despair and Christian Faith*, S.C.M. Press, 1941.

marriage preparation which could not be done by an experienced and theologically educated layman, so the kind of rules which many bishops wisely lay down with regard to the minimum length of time in the priesthood for hearing confessions need not apply.

Experienced clergy, with an understanding of the theology of marriage and an ordinary knowledge of people, should not hesitate to undertake this work, even though themselves unmarried. In an ideal parish it might be possible for the unmarried clergyman to arrange for each couple to spend an evening with a happily married Christian husband and wife in order to discuss with them any and every aspect of married life. Indeed such informal getting together and talking among lay people can be most fruitful. But it should be supplementary to the main preparation by the parish priest, not a substitute for it.

We may give full weight to Dr Vidler's point already quoted, and still believe that the married clergyman is in a better position to undertake this particular service. Not that the mere fact of being married is a sufficient qualification. It would probably be wise to suggest that a young and newly married curate should not embark on marriage preparation for a year or two. Every couple takes time to become adjusted to the changes which marriage brings, and the clergy are no exception. Indeed there are some marriages which never appear to settle down to run smoothly and harmoniously, and again the clergy are like others and face this risk. It must be exceedingly difficult to give advice to others if one's own marriage and home life is not a happy one.

The fact that most parishes, when there is a vacancy, ask for a married man is an indication of the popular image of the clerical household. Over eighty per cent of incumbents in the Church of England are married, and the debt the parishes owe to this fact is enormous. The chief part of it is not the provision of a full-time, though unpaid, woman worker, but the existence of a home at the centre of the parish where an attempt is made to put into practice the ideals of Christian marriage. Where this is not the case, the whole of a man's ministry suffers immeasurably.

It follows that the choice of a life partner is of great significance in the life and ministry of a clergyman. Nowadays the general tendency is towards early marriages, and this includes the clergy. Indeed Principals of Theological Colleges have been known to complain that the young men of today regard Holy Matrimony as a sacrament generally necessary to salvation. This being so, more thought should be given in the colleges to teaching about the kind of life to which a clergyman's wife is called. Nor should we shrink from telling young ordinands of the importance of their choice. I have quoted elsewhere some words of a former bishop of Durham:

> Let the true man, who is at present free in respect of marriage-engagements, resolve that in the whole question of seeking or not seeking a wife he will consider first, midst, and last his Master's work, his Master's ministry. Better a thousand times be the most solitary of human beings than choose with your eyes open a married life in which you will not find positive help (not merely no positive hindrance) in your work for the Lord Jesus Christ.[1]

In no part of his work is a priest's own home life more influential than in his preparation of couples for marriage. Whether his wife takes an active part in the preparation or not, she is a vital factor in the whole process. In most Theological Colleges some attempt is made to help those wives and fiancées who are able to attend a week-end for training, or a series of talks. But this can only be on a voluntary basis, and is far from adequate. Is it not time that the Church took seriously the task of training its clergy wives?

Of equal importance with the right choice of a wife is the

[1] *The Ordinal*, Hodder & Stoughton, 1964. The full quotation on pp. 120, 121 of *The Ordinal* is from *To My Younger Brethren*, written in 1891 by Handley Moule when he was still Principal of Ridley Hall. The chapters appeared in serial form in *The Clergyman's Magazine*, and were subsequently published as a book by Hodder & Stoughton.

training of the children. It is pitiable for a priest to be exhorting others to bring up their children for God if his own family is in rebellion. I can only repeat what I wrote in *The Ordinal*:[1]

> The bringing up of children is no easier for the clergyman than for the lay Christian. There is indeed a danger that, in giving time to his parish morning, noon and night he may give too little attention to his own family. Children of a clerical household do not automatically grow up as good Christians. Prayer and example are the two biggest factors. A forced religion, or unnatural piety, will only repel. But if children grow up in the atmosphere of love and joyful Christian service they will respond. On the other hand they are quick to recognise the slightest insincerity.

The considerations in this chapter lead us to answer the question of its title thus. Every parish priest should consider it his privilege to do this work, and should equip himself for it by every available means. But more important by far than any technical skill is the quality of his own marriage, home, and family life, which in turn is dependent on the depth of his spiritual commitment.

[1] Ibid., p. 122.

4

Where To Begin

It is conceivable that at some time in our ministry we shall have to marry a couple whom we have not seen until the eve of the wedding. This is highly unsatisfactory, but it is no good refusing to do it when an emergency, such as the bridegroom's embarkation leave, makes it necessary. In such cases we just have to do the best we can. Normally we shall expect to see the couple together well in advance of the marriage. We can then make arrangements to see them again nearer the time, either once or for a series of talks according to the method we choose to adopt. In a large parish, where it becomes known that on certain Saturdays in the year there will be a number of weddings, the first contact may be made six months, or even a year, in advance. But is six months adequate time for us to help people to prepare? Is an interview, or series of interviews, a month or two before the day, the best we can do?

In many instances it is *all* we can do. There are the cases where people come to us with whom we are not in touch as regular, or even occasional, church-goers. We do what we can, and seize the opportunity with both hands. But there is a barrier to be broken down before we can hope to get through. It is far better if we already know the couple through previous contact. For if they have been linked to a church youth organization, they will, or should, have had quite a bit of preparation for marriage already.

For one thing the Church does a great service to young people by bringing them together in an atmosphere where the sexes mix naturally. Separate organizations for boys and girls have their place, but over a certain age we ought to provide the opportunities for them to get together. The vicar was speaking more truly than he realized when he announced on Sunday: "The Scouts and Guides will meet as usual during the week." Mixed youth groups, properly run, have everything to commend them. Their object and programme lie outside the scope of this volume, but we recognize their value in inculcating a right attitude to the opposite sex. They should encourage an atmosphere where it is possible to be friends with all without becoming exclusive with any, where boy-girl friendships can begin—and end—without too much notice being taken either way, and where anything like "petting" is known to be "out" by general consensus of opinion.

Leadership of such a group is the key to the situation. It is essential that the leaders be dedicated Christians. Ideally a young married couple is most suitable, but the prior claim of a family makes this seldom realizable. Whoever leads must be young enough in spirit to have the confidence of youth, and old enough to be firm when necessary. Their biggest contribution is in creating the right spirit. But in addition they will introduce into the programme, from time to time, subjects directly connected with boy-girl relationships. The more naturally such matters are treated as part of the whole concept of the Christian life the better.

As an example of what can be done I commend *Training the Youth Group*[1] by Derek Tasker. It contains three courses, "The Christian at Home", "The Christian and his Job", and "The Use of our Spare Time". These are very practical subjects, and all are related to the teaching of the Bible. "The Christian at Home" includes studies on "Parents", "Courting", "The Marriage Service", "What is different about a Christian Home?", and "Bachelors and Spinsters". But it *starts* with a study on "What the Bible has to say about Sex, Marriage, and Family-life". In the context of the Christian

---

[1] A. R. Mowbray, 1960.

life as a whole this is seen in its proper perspective. Probably Derek Tasker is right when he says:

> Few of our young people have begun to realise that God has something to say about sex—apart from a few negative prohibitions. This is one of the chief reasons why they are bowled over by contemporary influences. There is a vacuum which we have failed to fill.

This vacuum must be filled well before a couple comes to put up the banns, and the role of the youth group is vital.

However good may be the lay leadership of the work among young people, it is important that the clergy should be associated with it too. In particular they should know the kind of message which is being put across, and to a greater or lesser extent share in giving it. If the parson is never heard speaking to the young people about such a subject as "Friendship, Love, and Marriage", they may get the impression that these things are more suitable to be dealt with by laymen, and that the clergy are only concerned with more "spiritual" matters —a double error if ever there was one. From time to time a sermon in church on the subject might be followed by questions put to a panel of which the preacher is one of the members.

In Confirmation classes, the supreme occasion for systematic teaching of the faith and practice of a Christian, the subject of friendship between the sexes must be dealt with positively. Harm can be done if the Seventh Commandment is made the opportunity merely for a tirade against sexual sin. We certainly should not hesitate to deal with the need, in the words of the Revised Catechism, "to be clean in thought, word, and deed, controlling my bodily desires through the power of the Holy Spirit who dwells within me; and if called to the state of marriage, to live faithfully in it". That is finely said, and needs saying. But we ought also to teach positively about the sanctity of marriage, and let young people know that the reason jokes about sex are "out" is not that it is a nasty subject but that it is too sacred a matter to be so treated.

In reality the whole of life is preparation for marriage; for if we can make good Christians, we have the material of which Christian marriages, homes, and families can be built. The direct influence of the clergy on the children and young people of the parish varies considerably; though indirectly, through the encouragement of Christian teachers in schools, and of parents in their own homes, we are called to contribute a great deal. Each generation is largely made by the homes in which the children grow up. This is part of our difficulty today. The young people who are coming to us to get married have very little Christian background, and for this their parents must receive at least some of the blame. We have to take them where we find them, and try to lead them to lay the foundations of a Christian home. If that happens, there is more hope for the generation to come.

Sometimes it seems like a vicious circle, and we do not see where we can break in. The truth is that there is no part of our ministry which is not connected with the whole, and the pastoral care we give to the parents of a baby brought to Baptism may well be the first step in preparing that baby for marriage in twenty-five years' time. It is not possible to say where we begin. It is certain that we never stop.

5

Whom Can We Marry?

I suggested in chapter 1 that we should not refuse to marry those who come to us, even if they are not regular church-goers. That this is the historic practice of the Church of England there is no doubt, and though there are voices raised against such "indiscriminate" giving of the Church's blessing, the vast majority of the clergy take this non-rigorist line. But in fact the marriages we are permitted to solemnize are not so indiscriminate as the word might imply. There are some very strict limitations.

First there is the Table of Kindred and Affinity printed at the end of the Prayer Book. It is based on the prohibitions of Leviticus 18 and in its original form was issued by Archbishop Parker in 1563. Canon 99 of 1603 ordered that "the aforesaid Table shall be in every church publicly set up and fixed at the charge of the parish". It was not until the present century that an Act of Parliament was passed allowing marriage with a deceased wife's sister, and even then a clause of the Act excluded interference with ecclesiastical custom. But when someone who had so married was excluded from Holy Communion, the courts pronounced the action illegal and the House of Lords upheld that judgement. The present position and the Table as now printed in the Prayer Book are governed by an amendment to the Canon made in 1946.

The Table of Kindred and Affinity is mainly of academic interest, and if ever a case should arise about which there were some doubt, it would be well to refer it to the Bishop, whose legal advisers would decide what should be done.

3

There may be occasions when a marriage is proposed between first cousins. This is perfectly legal as they are related only to the fourth degree, that is to say they are both two generations removed from a common ancestor. But while there is no legal barrier there may be some doubt about the wisdom of such a couple having children. This subject is not strictly within the province of the priest, but he may feel it right to suggest that the couple should talk to a doctor who would explain to them any possible risk to the health of the children. Much would depend on the medical record of the family.

We are also legally prohibited from allowing the marriage of a couple in the parish church unless one of them lives in the parish or is on the electoral roll. It is important that these requirements should be observed *bona fide*. A non-resident may be on the electoral roll of a parish church in which he or she has habitually attended public worship for the past six months. The word "habitually" is difficult to define but it ought to be interpreted in such a way as to mean genuine membership of the congregation. The residential qualifications should also be strictly enforced. It is intended that people should be married in the church of the parish where one of them actually lives, unless as already mentioned one or other is on the electoral roll of another parish. In this latter case the banns must be called in the parish or parishes in which the couple reside, as well as in the parish in which the marriage is to take place.

In practice the question of residence gives rise to a good many problems. Technically the place of residence is where one is living during the three Sundays on which the banns are called. (Not, of course, that the three Sundays need necessarily be consecutive.) But often young people are living away from home. If their parents' home is the place to which they normally come back, then they can be counted as residents. The main difficulty is over those who want to establish residential qualifications in order to be married in the church of a parish other than their own. If the law is to be kept, the party concerned must spend more than half the fifteen days in residence, which really amounts to spending eight nights at the given address. It is difficult to see how less can be demanded, and the practice of permitting the bride or bridegroom to leave a suitcase at an address in the parish in the belief that this constitutes "residence" seems uncommonly like evasion. Perhaps the whole principle of the calling of banns is no longer an effective way of achieving the object originally intended. Banns remain in force for three months, after which, if the wedding has for some reason been postponed, they must be called again.

An alternative to marriage after banns is marriage by licence. This is merely a licence to dispense with the calling of banns. It is useful in cases where there is not time to have the banns called, or when a couple, for perfectly good reasons, want to avoid the publicity of banns. A couple wanting a licence should be directed to the nearest surrogate.[1] Contrary to a commonly held belief, a licence does not dispense with the ordinary qualifications of either residence or membership of the electoral roll. The only way in which a couple can be married at any time or place in England without previous residence is by obtaining a *special* licence. This is issued in special circumstances by the Archbishop of Canterbury and costs £25. Confusion sometimes arises through people speaking of a "special licence" when what they mean is simply a "licence", the cost of which is not so prohibitive.[2]

The legal age for marriage is 16. If, however, either of the

[1] A surrogate is a clergyman appointed by the Bishop to receive applications for licences. The statements are sworn in his presence and he forwards these to the Diocesan Registrar who actually issues the licence. A list of Surrogates is published in the Diocesan Year Book.

[2] Application for a special licence is made to the Registrar of the Court of Faculties, 1 The Sanctuary, Westminister, S.W.1. It is given only in exceptional circumstances, e.g. when a marriage is desired in a College Chapel which is not licensed for marriage, or in grave emergencies. The Bishop of Sodor and Man has the right of granting special licences for marriage in the Isle of Man.

parties is under 21, the consent of the parents or guardians is necessary. Legally consent is assumed unless it is specifically withdrawn. It is, however, advisable to have consent in writing and to file the letter with the form of application which the couple have filled in. Obviously, if a father is giving away his daughter who is under 21, we are safe in assuming that he is consenting to the marriage, but it is better to make no exceptions to the rule that written consent be given. When a licence is applied for, the surrogate will certainly require this.

If the consent of parents or guardians is withheld, minors may make application to the Courts, and if leave to marry is granted, the parish priest may face a pastoral problem. We have to try to encourage good relationships all round, and it may not be easy. Particularly if a couple is very young, even though the Court has granted permission for the marriage to take place, we may feel it right to press for delay. It is a matter of hard fact that the younger a couple is when they get married, the bigger the risk of a breakdown later (or even sooner). On the other hand we may have the task of persuading parents that they should not continue to oppose a marriage after the Court has overruled their previous refusal. I must say that I have almost always found parents very reasonable, sometimes even a little too reluctant to put their foot down when a certain amount of firmness would have been a good thing.

So far we have dealt with matters in which the law of the land and the law of the Church are largely in agreement. There are some other concerns which pose greater problems when we are considering whom we may marry in church. Legally we need not refuse to marry unbaptized persons, but the Church's tradition is against our doing so. Baptism, after all, is (in addition to much else) "a sign of profession, and mark of difference, whereby Christian men are discerned from others that be not christened" (Article XXVII). In theory, therefore, an unbaptized person may be assumed to belong to some other religion, and it would clearly be wrong to expect a Jew, for example, to take marriage vows in the Name of the Trinity in which he does not believe. In practice we know that many cases are not so simple. The unbaptized party—a Quaker or a member of the Salvation Army—might be more sincere in Christian belief than the person he or she was marrying, who happened to have been baptized but had never done much about it.

It seems unwise to have a rigid rule about never being willing to marry unbaptized persons. In most dioceses the Bishop requires to be consulted before such a marriage takes place. It is good to have the authority of the Bishop to fall back on, but he is bound to be guided by the facts of the case as put to him by the incumbent concerned. Briefly, what we have to be assured of is that both the parties sincerely desire a Christian marriage service and can conscientiously take part in it. We know that the fact of having been baptized is not an absolute guarantee of this, but the fact of *not* having been baptized does call for special dealing.

It might be thought that the obvious thing is to encourage the person in question to be baptized. This is indeed most desirable, but ought it not to be a matter of Baptism *and Confirmation*? To baptize an adult who has no intention of being confirmed and becoming a communicant seems to be wholly illogical. We must beware of a "Baptism of convenience", accepted simply to comply with an ecclesiastical ruling. But if a candidate is prepared to undergo instruction for Baptism and Confirmation, that is certainly the happiest solution.

The marriage of two Christians who belong to different denominations may not be ideal even in these days of ecumenicity. We should stress with them the desirability of worshipping together, and of bringing up their children, not merely on Christian principles but as worshipping members of the local church. The Roman Catholic Church has always seen this clearly and seeks, as a first preference, the "conversion" of the non-Roman Catholic party, or failing that, demands promises to the effect that all children of the marriage shall be brought up in the Roman Church. It will not countenance a marriage taking place except in a Roman Catholic church, and by a Roman Catholic priest. It is difficult to write on this subject at the present time, when there are hopes for some modification in Rome's attitude to mixed marriages. It is not too much to say that, as things have been up to the time of writing, the *ne temere* decree makes the position of the non-Roman partner very difficult, and we should teach our people clearly about this.[1]

Normally we shall not often find ourselves in the position of marrying a couple of whom one is a Roman Catholic. A devout Roman does not accept our ministrations and must regard himself, after a marriage service in the Church of England, as not truly married in the eyes of his own Church, and therefore presumably in the eyes of God. And a devout Roman would certainly not be prepared to "live in sin", which is what his position would amount to. We might conclude therefore that any Roman Catholic who was willing to be married in the Church of England must have thrown over his religion. But there is another possibility. There are those who have serious misgivings about the Faith in which they have been brought up, but who are nevertheless anxious to be Christians. We need not hesitate, from an over-scrupulous fear of proselytizing, to put before them the claims of the Church of England.

I have left to the end of this chapter on whom we may marry the consideration of the divorced person whose former husband or wife is still living. The State now allows divorce for a number of causes, and of course the right also to remarry. But the Matrimonial Causes Act of 1937 says that no clergyman can be compelled to solemnize the marriage of any

---

[1] Formerly the non-Roman party in a mixed marriage was required to sign a promise not to interfere with the religion of the other, and to allow all children of the marriage to be brought up as Roman Catholics. That this promise is now made verbally rather than in writing does not alter its nature for those who believe that a promise is a promise.

person whose former marriage has been dissolved otherwise than by death, or to permit the marriage to be solemnized in the church of which he is a minister. In other words we have the legal right to refuse. The question which some of the clergy find not so easy to answer is whether we have a moral right, or even duty, sometimes to conduct a marriage service in such a case.

The official answer of the Church, as expressed in an Act of Convocation in 1957, is no.[1] This does not mean that the Church can never recognize that a second marriage can take place while a former partner is still living. The gospel proclaims the forgiveness of sins, and we do not say that those who have remarried cannot be restored to fellowship in the Church. We have a very special responsibility for those whose marriages have failed. We must take people where we find them and win them for our Lord. While we were yet sinners Christ died for us, and there is no justification for excluding one particular kind of sinner. We must treat divorced people with all the love and compassion and caring with which our Lord will inspire us.

Why then can we not remarry divorcees in church? There are those who think we can, and should. They will call attention to the Matthaean exception and other New Testament teaching which seems to admit the possibility of remarriage after divorce for certain causes. Others feel that a rigid rule savours of an unchristian legalism and that the application of Christian *principles* calls for changed attitudes in view of changed circumstances. Fewer people than formerly are prepared to distinguish too precisely between the innocent and the guilty party: nevertheless there *are* cases where one party is notoriously sinned against and there seems to be no alternative to divorce.

Yet the Church refuses consistently to marry any divorced person. Perhaps the key word is "consistently". It really is, in

[1] See Regulations Concerning Marriage and Divorce printed in full on pp. 28, 29.

the opinion of the present writer, the only consistent thing to do. Lord Fisher of Lambeth, when he was Archbishop of Canterbury, said:

> If the Church were to marry divorced persons, there would be no way left in which it could bear effective witness before the world to the standard of Christ, for there is no other official or formal act which would give it the opportunity.[1]

There will inevitably be the really hard cases, instances where the first marriage was a living hell, and the second marriage has been a veritable salvation. Are even such to be denied a church marriage? Let Lord Fisher speak again:

> Thus if they feel denial of a church marriage to be a "cross of suffering", they should bear it for the Church so that it may not, in its official acts of marrying, compromise the standard entrusted to it by our Lord, to defend which is the Church's essential duty.[2]

It would be foolish to pretend that all the clergy are convinced that the official position is the right one. It is our duty to think the matter out for ourselves, and if our conclusions are different from those at present accepted, work for a general change of attitude. The Church has received new insights in the past—as for example its change of mind about birth control—and it will do so again. Not that marriage will ever be other than God ordained it to be. But the Church's method of administering the discipline of Christ may change. Till it does, we do well to abide loyally by the standards which have been given us. It will be found in practice that difficulties arise less from those who are genuine "hard" cases than from those who desire a church wedding for less worthy reasons.

In any cases of doubt about whom we should marry it is well to consult the Diocesan Registrar. Advice may be needed where a party produces a certificate of nullity, which of course

[1] *The Archbishop Speaks*, Evans Brothers Limited, 1958, p. 148.
[2] Ibid., p. 151.

is quite different from a divorce, and is not a barrier to marriage. Other complicated cases may arise in the marriage of foreigners, and the Registrar may advise getting in touch with the appropriate Embassy or Consulate. Particular care should be taken also in the marriage of Service personnel to be sure that the consent of the particular authority has been obtained.

CONVOCATION OF CANTERBURY

REGULATIONS CONCERNING

MARRIAGE AND DIVORCE

Passed in the Upper House
on 16 May 1956 and 23 May 1957
and in the Lower House on 21, 22, and 23 May 1957,
and declared an Act of Convocation by
His Grace the Lord Archbishop of Canterbury
on 1 October 1957

1 "That this House reaffirms the following four Resolutions of 1938, and in place of Resolution 5 then provisionally adopted by the Upper House substitutes Resolution 2(A) below, which restates the procedure generally followed since 1938."

(1) "That this House affirms that according to God's will, declared by our Lord, marriage is in its true principle a personal union, for better or for worse, of one man with one woman, exclusive of all others on either side, and indissoluble save by death."

(2) "That this House also affirms as a consequence that remarriage after divorce during the lifetime of a former partner always involves a departure from the true principle of marriage as declared by our Lord."

(3) "That in order to maintain the principle of lifelong obligation which is inherent in every legally contracted marriage and is expressed in the plainest terms in the Marriage Service, the Church should not allow the use of that Service in the case of anyone who has a former partner still living."

(4) "That while affirming its adherence to our Lord's principle and standard of marriage as stated in the first and second of the

above resolutions, this House recognizes that the actual discipline of particular Christian Communions in this matter has varied widely from time to time and place to place, and holds that the Church of England is competent to enact such a discipline of its own in regard to marriage as may from time to time appear most salutary and efficacious."

2(A) "Recognizing that the Church's pastoral care for all people includes those who during the lifetime of a former partner contract a second union, this House approves the following pastoral regulations as being the most salutary in present circumstances:

(a) When two persons have contracted a marriage in civil law during the lifetime of a former partner of either of them, and either or both desire to be baptized or confirmed or to partake of the Holy Communion, the incumbent or other priest having the cure of their souls shall refer the case to the Bishop of the diocese, with such information as he has and such recommendations as he may desire to make.

(b) The Bishop in considering the case shall give due weight to the preservation of the Church's witness to Our Lord's standard of marriage and to the pastoral care of those who have departed from it.

(c) If the Bishop is satisfied that the parties concerned are in good faith and that their receiving of the Sacraments would be for the good of their souls and ought not to be a cause of offence to the Church, he shall signify his approval thereof both to the priest and to the party or parties concerned: this approval shall be given in writing and shall be accepted as authoritative both in the particular diocese and in all other dioceses of the province."

2(B) "No public Service shall be held for those who have contracted a civil marriage after divorce. It is not within the competence of the Convocations to lay down what private prayers the curate in the exercise of his pastoral Ministry may say with the persons concerned, or to issue regulations as to where or when these prayers shall be said."

2(C) "Recognizing that pastoral care may well avert the danger of divorce if it comes into play before legal proceedings have been started, this House urges all clergy in their preparation of couples for marriage to tell them, both for their own sakes and for that of their friends, that the good offices of the clergy are always available."

The following Resolution was passed by the Lower House of the Convocation of Canterbury on 2 October 1957:

> This House desires to place on record its warm support of the action of His Grace the President in promulgating as an Act of Convocation the Resolutions of Convocation on Marriage and Divorce, and His Grace's statement which accompanied it; respectfully requests the President to ensure that this Act be made well known in each Diocese; and calls upon the clergy of the Province to give to the Act their loyal and unstinted allegiance in word and deed.

6

The First Approach

First impressions are always important. The kind of reception a couple gets when they come to put up the banns may well colour the rest of our dealings with them, and the extent to which they will be responsive to what we have to offer. We need to remember that this is not a casual call or the result of a hasty decision to go and see the vicar. They have reached a critical moment in their lives when they want to fix the date. They are naturally a bit excited, even nervous. If they are not regular church-goers, or in some other way known to us, there is the additional strain of an interview with a clergyman, which may seem to them quite alarming. Our first concern must be to put them at their ease and make them feel that we welcome them.

How we deal with the first approach about arranging a wedding will vary according to the size of the parish. What is possible in a small parish where half a dozen marriages in the year would be a maximum, or even in the moderately large parish where thirty or forty in the year may be considered an average number, would be quite out of the question in one of those populous areas where there may be two or three hundred weddings a year and even a dozen or more on a single day at the appropriate season (which may have more to do with Income Tax than with the Church's Year). In such cases there would be sheer chaos if couples were to call at the vicarage at any odd time in the hope of finding the vicar at home and free to see them. Some system must be devised whereby one of the clergy is known to be available at certain times, and when these times are announced they must unfailingly be kept.

In these very large parishes it may be necessary for the first approach to be made to the verger, or to the parish secretary if there is one. Where this is the case it is essential that such people should be members of the team with the incumbent and other clergy, and see their function as a part of the ministry of the Church. One advantage of seeing the verger first is that some couples, who are overawed by the thought of going to the vicar, are less shy about going to a lay official. But there are disadvantages too. If they come straight to us, we can begin to build up confidence from the first. There are things we can say to them at the very first meeting. And we avoid giving the impression, so fatal in pastoral work, that the clergyman is the V.I.P. who can only be approached through lesser mortals.

In the average parish there should be no great difficulty in arranging for all to see the vicar in the first instance. It can be made known, through the magazine and notice board, that he is at home between certain times on certain days; or that appointments may be made by 'phone; or whatever method suits the parish best. We want the kind of efficient planning which enables us to let people see that we have plenty of time for them, and are not anxious to hurry off to the next engagement. This is sometimes difficult, and we may not always be able to help keeping people waiting in another room while we finish talking with the couple before them. But the atmosphere of the waiting-room is to be avoided. Business-like arranging of our engagements is in order to give a feeling of leisure while we talk to people, not to give the impression of being busy and self-important.

The best place for couples to come, even for their first visit to put up the banns, is to the clergyman's home. Circumstances may make it necessary to use the vestry or parish office instead, but it must be regarded as a second-best. It goes without saying that whoever opens the front door asks the couple in straight away. The first words are not "What can I do for you?" but "Do come in." A vicar's wife who can make a young couple feel that of all the people in the world they are the ones she is most pleased to see at that moment is doing a great service for the Kingdom of God. The couple is brought into the study, and asked to sit down. Where? Not on two upright chairs placed so that the vicar looks at them across his desk from his own upright chair. Not even (at least I give this as my opinion) on two easy chairs side by side. No, they sit together on the sofa, that essential piece of study furniture for any clergyman who is going to do marriage preparation work. They may very likely begin by sitting on the edge, but as we relax in an armchair (rather than sitting at our desk) they will begin to respond and feel more at ease.

This is only the preliminary meeting, and if some prefer to keep it on a more strictly business level, they must do what they think right. My own strongly held conviction is in favour of informality, which need not mean any sacrifice of efficiency. For there is business to be done and we need not spend too long on pleasantries.

The most important business is all dealt with on the form which has to be filled in. There are standard forms obtainable from the S.P.C.K., but some dioceses and parishes prefer to print their own. All the details required for the marriage register must be entered: names, ages, condition, occupation, address, fathers' names and occupations. It is not unknown for people to be stumped by "condition", which of course is bachelor or widower, spinster or widow. It is not an inquiry into the state of the couple's health. Other questions that should be answered refer to the length of time that each has lived at the address given, whether there is any relationship, whether there has been a previous marriage not terminated by death, and of course the date and time of the wedding.

All these items are usually quite straightforward, though under the heading of occupation one gets an insight into the amazing variety of ways in which people earn their living.

Under father's name the name of the legal father should be entered, not that of a step-father. In the case of an illegitimate child who has been legally adopted it should be the legal father, not the actual father even if his name is known. When an illegitimate child is brought up by his or her unmarried mother, the mother's name can be entered in this column, or the space can be left blank.

The filling up of the form is the opportunity for establishing that *bona fide* residential qualifications exist. It should be explained that the banns must be put up also in the parish of the other party and that a banns certificate must be obtained and brought or sent before the wedding can take place. Where a marriage is being solemnized by virtue of an electoral roll qualification, the banns must also be published in the parishes in which both bride and bridegroom reside. If these things are not made clear to the couple at an early stage, there is danger that they may be overlooked and necessitate a last-minute rush to obtain a licence. Some couples imagine that in any case they need a licence, or must notify the registrar, and we can explain that a clergyman of the Church of England is empowered to carry through all the legal side of the marriage.

In busy parishes it is not always possible to fit a wedding in at the time, or even on the date, asked for. If people fix up the reception first and then find that the church is not free when they want it, they have only themselves to blame. Not of course that we shall tell them so, however strong the temptation. We need to let it be known that, while we do our best to accommodate a wedding at the time desired, there are other demands on the use of the church and on the minister's time. The prevalent custom of having weddings on a Saturday is what makes the congestion. Ideally there should be an hour between the beginning of each wedding if proper time is to be given for one lot of guests to depart and the next to arrive. At that rate it is possible to fit ten services into the statutory times of 8 a.m. to 6 p.m.

Parishes have their own rules about whether they will allow weddings in Lent or on Sundays. Strictly speaking we cannot legally refuse to marry on any day in the year, though we are allowed to choose the time at which we are free to do so. In this way we can make it clear that we disapprove of weddings, for instance, in Holy Week. It is not a very good plan to charge extra for a wedding on a Sunday. The word "overtime" is not in the priest's vocabulary, and we must avoid giving the impression that we will do for money what we would not do otherwise. It is best to be reasonable in meeting the desires of those who come to us, never forgetting that it is their big day and that, for them, everything else revolves round their wedding. I can remember a Christmas Day wedding, at the end of the usual long succession of services, which was not very popular with the vicarage family, and presumably with the organist and verger as well.

At the first interview it may transpire that one of the parties is divorced. If the Church's official line is taken (see pages 25–6), the case must be put with the utmost care. We must explain that our refusal to solemnize such a marriage is in the interests of the divine institution itself, and that we cannot compromise a principle in order to meet a hard case. But we must offer to help in any way we can, which may include a private service of prayer either in the home or in church. If the latter, it should not be a kind of mock wedding, with bridesmaids and guests, but a simple service of prayer strictly confined to those who want to pray with the couple. The way in which the Church's attitude is expressed may make all the difference to the future of those whose previous marriage has foundered, and who genuinely desire a new start in Christ.

Practical matters need to be arranged at this preliminary interview. The couple should be told about the fees. These are fixed by law and a table of fees is supposed to be displayed in the porch or vestry of every parish church. Most couples do not want to know all the details about how the fees are made

up, or how much goes to incumbent, clerk, and P.C.C. At
present (1966) for a wedding service without music the total
cost, including previous publication of banns and the provision of one marriage certificate, is the very reasonable sum
of £2 14s. 3d. Most couples want music, and this doubles the
fees all round, and of course there is an additional fee for
the organist and for the choir. In some churches there is a
charge for the bells, and there may be other extras such as
additional flowers, red carpet, and so on. Whatever is required
of the various services offered should be booked when the
first arrangements are made, and entered in the diary.

Some couples may want a friend to play the organ for their
wedding. We have to explain that this can only be by permission of the regular organist, who must receive his usual
fee even if someone else plays. Similarly, if a visiting clergyman is to be asked to take the service, it must be with the
incumbent's permission, or indeed, strictly speaking, at his
invitation; and again the incumbent receives the fee. If a
couple wants to make private arrangements about flowers,
care must be taken that the regular people in charge of
flowers are consulted.

The details of the service may be left to the main interview,
including the choice of hymns, unless these are required well
in advance for printing on a service paper. Guidance in the
choice of hymns will be discussed later.[1] If a service sheet is to
be printed, it is important that a draft is shown to the clergyman before it goes to the printer. It is handy to have some
specimens to show to the couple so that they will know the
form such service papers take in that particular church.
Generally speaking it is wise to have everything printed which
has to be said or sung by the congregation, including the
Gloria after the Psalm, and the Versicles and Responses. The
words of the hymns should be taken from the hymn book in

[1] See pp. 43-4.

4

use in that church, otherwise we are apt to find the choir singing "Alleluia" while the congregation sing "Praise Him,
praise Him". It can be explained that service papers are by
no means essential, and that hymn books and prayer books or
service booklets can be given out instead.

Other details in which the co-operation of the clergy may
be sought are concerned with photographs and tape-recordings. There can be no objection to the wedding photos being
taken outside the church or, one would imagine, in the vestry
after the registers have been signed. Differences of opinion
arise when it comes to photographing the actual service. Some
will not allow it in any circumstances. Others permit such
photographs provided the photographer is out of sight and
there is no noise, as there might be from a cine-camera. Very
much the same two attitudes are taken to tape-recordings.
Eminent churchmen have pronounced them unsuitable, and
if there is an episcopal ruling on the subject in a diocese, it
should be respected. But the reason for the objection is difficult to see. I can conceive the possibility of an occasion when
the playing back of the recording of the vows might help to
heal a rift in the marriage, and surely the happiest of marriages could only be made happier by husband and wife hearing over again the words and music which perhaps they only
partially took in at the time. In these days when all kinds of
religious services are televised there ought to be some second
thoughts about such matters.

If the couple should raise the question of confetti, it is well
to quote the Litter Act of 1958 which made it illegal to throw
it in the street. Unsuitable in the Church, illegal in the street,
there really is no excuse for the continuance of this rather
stupid custom. Vergers who sweep up the churchyard after a
wedding would certainly like to see the end of it.

Before this preliminary interview ends, the date must be
fixed for the main session or sessions in preparation for the
marriage. In the next chapter we discuss when and how this

is to be done. At the first meeting we have simply got a good deal of business out of the way, and made friendly contact. We may go on to speak of general topics, including the question of where they are going to live. As often as not they have not found anywhere yet.

Choosing The Method

The first wedding I ever took was disastrous. I had gone to take Morning Prayer at a church where the vicar was away. On arrival I was informed that there was a wedding to follow. Hadn't the vicar told me? He certainly had not. I was a deacon at the time and, though legally entitled to marry, ecclesiastically quite unprepared to do so. I had been best man at two weddings and been present, as far as I can remember, at one other in my life. Christian Worship lectures in college had not told me anything about the *conduct* of the services, nor had I ever been shown how to take a wedding. I got through somehow, probably in my nervousness giving blessings which I had no authority to give. I may even have given an impromptu address. I cannot remember. The couple may have lived happily ever after, but if so it was not the Church's doing. They were as unprepared as I was. The congregation was large and noisy. Not all the alcoholic refreshment had been kept till after the service. No doubt everybody voted it a fine occasion, and we sang the hymn which the happy pair had chosen. It was "Fight the good fight with all thy might".

I am not exaggerating. These things happened. That they happened to me, who thirty-six years later am called upon to write a book on marriage preparation, is part of the irony of fate. The fact that I can head this chapter "Choosing the Method" is an indication that things are very different to-day. Here and there we might still find a survival of the bad old days. But for the most part the only question is how best to do this work which we know to be vital. When the couple have come to put up the banns and we have discussed the arrangements as outlined in the last chapter, how are we to set about the business of the final preparation? What method shall we choose?

Whatever the method, we need to begin in good time, certainly not less than a month before the wedding. Six months would be too long: the couple would have had time to forget some of the things we had told them. A fortnight is definitely too short, for when last-minute arrangements are being made, their minds may be too full of other things to be able to give serious attention to the most important matters of all. Somewhere between two months and one month before the marriage is about right. In our talks we may want to suggest the reading of a book, a medical check-up, a visit to the Family Planning Clinic, or other things which could not be fitted in if the interview came only a few days before the wedding.

A method which is well-tried, and has proved successful, is to have one fairly long session in which the couple and the priest go through the whole of the marriage service and all the many points which it raises. If this method is adopted, then care must be taken to leave adequate time. When an interview is arranged for 8 o'clock it is no use having another appointment that same evening. By the time 9 o'clock comes the couple—and the priest—will be ready for a cup of coffee or tea, and the session will go on for a long time after that. This single long interview may be the best in most cases, but there are drawbacks too. There may be too many ideas to digest on one evening, and if the talk gets off to a "sticky" start, it may be better to cut it short for that evening and take up the subject again at a second interview. On the other hand, with a really responsive couple there is a lot to be said for going on while the atmosphere is helpful to the reception of ideas.

A modification of the two session method is to have a long interview in the study and a shorter one, much nearer the time, in the church. This can be a kind of rehearsal to make sure that bride and bridegroom know where to stand and what to say and do. It gives the opportunity to reinforce the significance of the vows and the prayers. To finish such a rehearsal with a short act of worship, in which thanksgiving, penitence, and commitment all find a place, is a natural step which is usually welcomed. But if we have an interview in the study and a rehearsal at the church, we must be careful to avoid giving the impression that any part of marriage is more, or less, sacred than any other.

When the priest is a married man, there is the possibility of his wife taking some part in the preparation sessions. One method is for the clergyman to see the couple together first, then talk with the man on his own while his wife talks with the woman, and finally see them together again. No doubt there are things which can best be said man to man and woman to woman, but not everyone cares to discuss things affecting their marriage except with the other present. This is particularly so in the matter of sex. It might be possible for the clergyman's wife to be present and take part in the whole of the session, but some couples would find this more inhibiting than seeing the clergyman alone. I think the wife should certainly meet the couple, at the "tea break" for instance, and they should be made to feel that they are welcome guests in the home. Domestic happiness does not need to be talked about, but where it is genuine it can be infectious.

Another method that is frequently used, particularly in parishes which have a large number of weddings, is preparation in groups. If the groups are too large, say more than four or five couples, such preparation can be little more than a lecture, or series of lectures, and this is not very desirable. Where there can be no come-back from those we are trying to help, we are not likely to get very far. "Responsive counselling" is the important thing. And it may well be that in *small* groups there can be more response than with an individual couple. After the preliminary shyness has been overcome they give each other confidence. Ideas which they would hestitate to mention if they were on their own do not appear so outrageous when they find that others share them.

This kind of group preparation is used in the courses offered to engaged couples by the National Marriage Guidance Council. They are held in the home of a married couple who are both trained in this work, and who run the evening strictly as discussions rather than talks. They are there to guide, but not to direct. The whole range of married life is covered in the course of four evenings, usually at weekly intervals. Where such courses are available, the priest may well feel that he should advise couples to attend them. This should not be a substitute for his own talks with the couple, but a valuable addition to them. The Marriage Guidance Council is not specifically Christian, though it accepts the Christian and Jewish ideals of marriage as its basis, and many of its counsellors, as would be expected, are convinced and practising Christians. We should co-operate with them in the work of marriage preparation as much as we can, and it may be that we shall be able to recommend suitable couples in our congregation to be trained for this work.

Even where Marriage Guidance Council courses are not available, or where a priest prefers to keep the preparation directly under the Church's umbrella, the group method may be found the best. It might be a case of choosing between giving an evening to each of four couples separately, or four evenings to the four couples together. It is a difficult decision to make. I think myself that something would be lost if we did not have time to see each couple by themselves at least once. And while the discussion technique is excellent, provided we know how to use it, there is room as well for definite instruction.

For instruction purposes some find it helpful to use a film strip. It really depends on whether the clergyman is happy with the technique of this particular method or not, and also on the level of intelligence of those we are preparing. While a film strip could be used with one couple, it is probably better suited to a small group, and is likely to give rise to subsequent discussion. Twenty minutes' instruction with the aid of a film strip could spark off a whole evening's profitable conversation. This would necessitate at least four evenings. The particular film strip I know best is called *Your Marriage*, and is based on my own book with the same title,[1] though I can take no credit (nor accept any blame) for the pictorial presentation. There are four strips, about 220 frames in all, and evidently many parishes find them useful.[2]

It must be left to each priest to work out a method which may well be a combination of some of the suggestions here made. Whatever we propose to do will be made plain to the couple at the preliminary interview, and dates fixed accordingly. The most elaborate preparation could consist of four group discussions, each introduced by a film strip talk, an interview with the couple alone, and a rehearsal in church. In many parishes there would not be time for all this in the weekly programme, and not all couples would welcome such a heavy dose. As we go on to discuss the kind of things we want to get across to those we marry, we shall take them in the order in which they arise in the marriage service. Whatever the method, this is the basis of our teaching, but by giving it in the form of a commentary on the service I am not suggesting that this is the only way. As in our Confirmation classes we can teach the Faith on the basis of the Catechism without making the bones of the skeleton too prominent, so we can say all that needs to be said about marriage from the Solemnization of Matrimony, using the points in the service merely as pegs on which to hang our teaching.

[1] *Your Marriage*, Hodder & Stoughton, 1958.
[2] Church Pastoral-Aid Society, Falcon Court, 32 Fleet Street, London E.C.4; or available through S.P.C.K. bookshops.

8

The Choice Of Hymns

Hymns may be chosen at the preliminary interview, or may be the first topic discussed at the main session. They are a very important part of the service and a couple may well want advice over the choice. We need to be careful how we turn down the suggestion of a hymn we may think quite unsuitable. Undoubtedly we may sometimes have to do so, but some choices which appear quite hopeless may turn out to be right in the circumstances. The hymn for those in peril on the sea, which could scarcely be more inappropriate for most weddings, would be thoroughly suitable if the bridegroom were a seaman. Favourite hymns sometimes have very special associations, and we must be gentle in the treatment we give them. But I have headed off "Abide with me" before now, and a number of others equally unfitting to the occasion.

We need to ask the couples what ideas they want to express in the first moments of the wedding service. Is it to be thanksgiving? Then what about "Praise, my soul, the King of heaven", or some other hymn of praise? What could be finer than "For the beauty of the earth?" Or perhaps they want to express their sense of dependence on God. This feeling accounts for the most frequent choice of all, "Lead us, heavenly Father, lead us", though the second verse contains some rather unfortunate lines (our Lord was not "dreary", nor was the world an unrelieved "desert" for him any more than it is for us). But the habit of choosing it will not be easily broken. Any hymn which brings the congregation reverently before God in worship makes a splendid opening. Such is

"Holy, Holy, Holy! Lord God Almighty", a completely objective hymn which mentions man only once—in the line, "Though the eye of sinful man thy glory may not see".

The final hymn may be one of dedication. Such is "Love divine, all loves excelling". It is often chosen, probably because the first line suggests the beauty of human love. This is not wrong, but we need to show that the hymn is addressed to our Lord himself, asking him to come and do his saving work in our lives. Some of the hymns specially written for weddings are prayers for the newly married couple, and come best at the end of the service. Such are "O perfect Love, all human thought transcending", and C. A. Alington's splendid verses, "O Father, by whose sovereign sway". Or the hymn of praise may be kept to the end, in which case "Now thank we all our God" can be recommended. These are only suggestions and there are many possibilities besides those that appear in hymn books under the heading of Holy Matrimony.

Sometimes a hymn is substituted for the Psalm in the middle of the service. The rubric in the 1928 service as amended and authorized in 1966 directs the saying or singing of a Psalm, and adds: "The following are suitable: 128; 67; 37.3–7". Presumably if a hymn is sung it should be one of the paraphrases of a Psalm, but I think I speak for many of the clergy if I say that *Crimond* might be given a rest. How fine it was when sung at the wedding of our Queen, when it came as a new and original idea. But over-familiarity has now destroyed its freshness.

When the hymns are being discussed it may also be appropriate to raise the subject of other music. The bride usually chooses what voluntary she would like when she walks up the church, and in a surprising number of cases she sticks to the traditional Wedding March. The discussion of these matters, important in themselves, helps to pave the way for other vital things as we hand the couple the Prayer Book, open at the Marriage Service, and prepare to think with them about the theology of marriage.

Now that the 1928 form of service is officially approved in the *Alternative Services First Series* (1966), there is a choice to be made between this and the service of 1662. Not many couples will be in a position to decide without some guidance. If our own preference is for the new service, we shall still need to explain the alternative vows and come to an agreement with the couple about which are to be used. As either alternative is equally permissible, we should not insist on our own preferences, though we can state the case for one or the other as we see it. The critical question is the inclusion or otherwise of the promise to obey. Incidentally if a couple asks for the 1662 service *in toto* we must presumably be ready to take it.

9

The Theology Of Marriage

"Now let's go over the details. It's your big day and we want it all to go without a hitch. I should like you, John, to arrive about a quarter of an hour before the service, with your best man of course. You will be shown to the vestry where you will check the entry in the register and the best man can settle the fees. At about five minutes to two I will show you to your seat in the front pew on the right, and then I shall go down to meet the bride. The bridesmaids will have arrived by this time, and we all wait till you, Mary, arrive—on the dot of two o'clock—and enter the church on your father's right arm. The organ begins the Wedding March, the congregation all stand, and you (John) and your best man come out of your pew and stand opposite the hassock placed for you on the chancel step. I lead the bride up the church, and when I turn round at the chancel step there you are in a straight line in front of me: the best man, the bridegroom, the bride, and the bride's father. Before we begin, Mary will turn round and give her bouquet to the chief bridesmaid. We sing the hymn and then I read the Introduction. This is what I want to look at now. It's addressed to the congregation, telling them what the Christian view of marriage is, and why you have come to church for your wedding."

Obviously this is not a speech to be learned by heart and recited. It is just an idea of the kind of approach we can adopt. We want to show that the service must be done decently and in order—that is the way God wants it—and, taking for granted that they are coming to church for the highest reasons, go on to explain what those reasons are.

No marriage can take place without witnesses. At least two are required to sign the register, whether in church or register office. There must always be a "congregation". But in church we declare that "we are gathered here in the sight of God" as well as "in the face of this congregation". Not indeed that God is absent from the register office, but his presence is not openly acknowledged. This Introduction declares that all that is to happen is done in the sight of God. He is the greatest witness of the marriage.

The purpose of our being there before God and the other witnesses is "to join together this man and this woman in Holy Matrimony". Here we are introduced to the real nature of marriage. The man and the woman are to be joined together. It is no mere partnership: it is a union. Because husband and wife are made one flesh, the union is permanent and exclusive. Hence the definition of marriage which a Christian accepts is: "The life-long union of one man and one woman, to the exclusion of all others." Nothing less than that is marriage in the sense in which a Christian understands it. This is Holy Matrimony. It is not holy because it is solemnized in church. On the contrary, it is solemnized in church because it is holy.

This honourable estate was instituted by God himself. Here is something basic to our understanding of the theology of marriage. In the words of J.-J. von Allmen.[1]

> Marriage is not an accidental but an essential element of creation, to the extent that man is himself, complete, capable of reflecting and displaying his Maker, only if he is "male and female" (Gen. 1:26f): it was not until the human couple had been formed that God was content with His work (Gen. 2:18).

Any understanding of the doctrine of Creation implies also the acceptance of marriage as part of the Divine Order. As I

[1] Article "Marriage" in *Vocabulary of the Bible*, Lutterworth Press.

have written elsewhere: "The fact of marriage as the divinely
ordained union of one man with one woman can no more
change than day and night, summer and winter, or any of the
other things that God has decreed."[1] If the 1662 Prayer Book
service is used, the words are: "instituted by God in the time
of man's innocency". The point is not as unimportant as
might be supposed. In the article already quoted von Allmen
says:

> By insisting on the fact that marriage was instituted before the
> appearance of sin Scripture contradicts every teaching which
> would see in the sexuality (or corporality) of man the disreput-
> able or shameful part of his being, and shows that from the very
> first it repudiates a dualistic conception of the world.

The truth of the divine institution of marriage may have
to be interpreted to the couple in the simplest terms. The
clearer we are in our own minds on the subject, the better able
shall we be to do this. Hence the need for a course of reading
for ourselves in order that we may be able to guide those who
come to us. But beware of presenting a couple with too much
of our own knowledge. Briefly, what we want to get over to
them is that marriage is an integral part of God's design for
the highest of his creatures, and that in itself it is something
utterly pure and beautiful. It is an honourable estate indeed.

Not only was marriage instituted by God, it is also spoken
of in the Bible as "signifying unto us the mystical union that
is betwixt Christ and his Church". With the not so well
initiated we may feel it necessary to omit this point or at best
to give it only a passing reference. It might be enough to say:
"You remember that in the Bible Christ is called the Bridegroom and the Church the Bride. This means that when
some way was needed to express the closeness of the union
between Christ and those who belong to him, no better illustration could be found than the union of husband and wife.
What an honour that places on marriage." Such simple words

---

[1] Parsons, op. cit., p. 13.

may be all that will be understood, even by some quite Christian couples.

But behind our explanation will lie our own deeper understanding of the biblical doctrine of the Church as the Bride of Christ. An excellent summary of this is given by Dr Alan Richardson in *An Introduction to the Theology of the New Testament*,[1] from which I quote:

> For the marriage-relationship is the deepest, richest and most satisfying personal human relationship of which we have experience; it is an experience of surrender without absorption, of service without compulsion, of love without conditions. In it are illustrated, as far as such realities can be illustrated by analogies within human experience, all the truths of God's love and grace in the lives of Christian disciples. To say that the Church is "one flesh" with Christ is to describe a structure of personal relationships in which the Christian disciple remains completely and utterly himself, yet finds himself developed into a "new man" through participation in the common life of Christ's body, the Church.

If such teaching is likely to pass over the heads of many couples we prepare for marriage, the same is not true of the reference to the wedding feast at Cana: "which holy estate Christ adorned and beautified with his presence, and first miracle that he wrought, in Cana of Galilee". Most people remember the story. We can point out that Christ's presence at the feast made it a more joyful occasion that it would otherwise have been. This may be a wholly new idea to some people whose conception of religion is of something negative and joyless. Christ is the Lord of all life, and shares in the happiness of life as well as in its sadness. And the changing of water into wine is a symbol of his power to change the ordinary into the extra-ordinarily good. Far too many marriages, even those that are apparently successful, become insipid for the lack of Christ's presence in the home. God does not mean life to be dull.

[1] S.C.M. Press, pp. 256–8.

Marriage is regarded in Scripture as the normal state. It is commended by St Paul (even though he, as far as we know, was unmarried) to be honourable among all men. There is no word "bachelor" in the Old Testament. Jeremiah's call to remain unmarried is a unique prophetic sign.[1] In the New Testament it is evident that some may be, for special purposes, called to a celibate life. But clearly marriage and a family are regarded as normal for most Christians. While there is nothing dishonourable about celibacy, whether voluntary or otherwise, the Prayer Book is absolutely right in its insistence that marriage is to be commended as honourable among all men. Such a high view of marriage ought to be a safeguard against its being entered upon for any but the highest reasons. To this subject we turn in our next chapter.

[1] Article on "Marriage" in *The New Bible Dictionary* (I.V.F.).

10

The Importance Of Being Sure

What would you think if you were the author of a book on marriage and were told by a clergyman who used it in his parish that he knew of two couples who had broken off their engagement through reading it? A first reaction might be similar to that of the writer of a work on Christian Apologetics finding that he had made a couple of his readers into atheists. But further reflection suggests other possibilities. Suppose—as was the case—the engagements that were broken were not really suitable. Is it not far better to make the discovery before it is too late? So, though before now I have almost pushed a bridegroom into going on with a marriage when, through nerves, he was hesitating, I can say "Thank God" when I hear that an engagement has been broken off before a marriage which would certainly be an unhappy one takes place. I am well aware that in the last analysis no one can be absolutely sure. There is always a risk when we embark on the unknown, though a Christian prefers to call it a step of faith. But everybody ought to be able to say, as they approach their wedding day, that they honestly believe they are doing the right thing.

It is not our business to try to unsettle anyone who has come to this conviction. We should assume that there is no doubt in their mind, and that what we have to say about wrong reasons for getting engaged will only help to confirm them in the rightness of their decision. Very often we find that doubts have occurred at some stage during the engagement, and have been resolved through mutual frankness and

5

understanding. So we shall not make too much of the dangers of a wrong choice, or encourage people to be over-introspective. All the same, a reminder of the way in which mistakes have sometimes been made does not come amiss at this stage. Marriage is a terribly serious business involving the absolute abandonment of each to the other. It is good to be sure that you are going to abandon yourself to the right person.

In the Introduction we read that because of what marriage is, it is "not by any to be enterprised, nor taken in hand, unadvisedly, lightly, or wantonly". These three words need to be discussed. I hope it is not dissembling, but rather being tactful, if we mention first one or two examples which could not possibly apply to the couple before us. For instance, if they are obviously about the same age, we could start by saying that a marriage between a man and a woman of vastly different ages might be unadvised. We can then go on to other things, which may or may not ring a bell with them; and if something does seem to apply, it can lead to a helpful discussion. Some of the factors which *may* make a marriage inadvisable, besides age, are health, race, colour, culture, religion. And if a marriage is literally "unadvised", that is to say if parents and others concerned are advising against it, there would certainly be causes for frank discussion of the situation. It is seldom right to be too dogmatic. There are exceptions to every rule. But at least it is good to get a couple to face the realities in what they are doing.

The second word is "lightly". Again we should assume that those who come to us have thought well about the seriousness of the step they are taking. Yet a few questions about how long they have known each other, in what circumstances, and how they first met, need not appear to be merely inquisitive. As to the first, I should prefer, not "How long have you known each other?" but "I expect you have known each other a long time, haven't you?" Generally they are only too pleased to go on and tell you all about it. The danger is not only that people have known each other too short a time, but that they have seen each other only in ideal circumstances. They ought to know each other in all moods, and above all in their homes. They have got to live together for a long time and they need a solid basis for their marriage. Mere infatuation will not do.

Which brings us to the third word, "wantonly". The 1662 service leaves no doubt about what this means: "to satisfy men's carnal lusts and appetites, like brute beasts that have no understanding". We ought to make it very clear to people that sex is important in marriage, but also that it is not everything. When sex is isolated from the rest of life, men and women are reduced to the level of animals. We need to tell people, in the words of Anne Proctor,

> that we are meant to enjoy the pleasures of sex, but that they are the consequence or reward (if you like) of facing our responsibilities. That the ideal of marriage to one partner for life is not a device to lessen the joys of sex, but is really the setting in which these joys can best be found. The Commandments are not there to say that the pleasures of physical love are wrong, but that those pleasures are likely to turn to dust and ashes if they are used without the steadying background which a permanent marriage brings.[1]

A permanent marriage is not likely to result if it is taken in hand "wantonly".

It is a relief to turn to the positive words which describe how marriage is to be undertaken: "reverently, discreetly, advisedly, soberly, and in the fear of God". Reverence is a word we associate with worship. Ought there not to be that element in the attitude to one another of those who are going to be married? In a former generation they used to speak of a couple who were getting friendly as *admiring* one another. Nowadays we should say they were getting fond of each other, which is a perfectly good way of putting it, but somehow the note of admiration is worth preserving. There ought to be

[1] *Background to Marriage*, Longmans, Green, p. 88.

a bit of awe and mystery about falling in love. We need to recover a sense of reverence for the whole subject of sex and marriage, for life itself, and especially for the other life with which we are to be united. If this is lacking today, perhaps it is because our generation has lost its reverence for God.

Part of our reverent approach to marriage will be our treating it "discreetly". The word suggests that we use our God-given power of choosing. It sounds a bit unromantic to suggest that we choose our life's partner, when all the world knows that what ought to happen is that you fall in love and that's that. But it isn't a bit as simple as that, and the marriage that will bring lasting happiness is the one where husband and wife have chosen each other with eyes open, having considered "soberly" all the factors. In the 1662 service the word "advisedly" is also included. This is hardly meant to suggest that a young man should go round his friends seeking advice about whom he should marry. But it is a very good sign if those who know him best and care for him most are wholehearted in their approval of his choice.

What will the average couple make of being told that marriage is to be undertaken "in the fear of God"? We may need to explain that it is not the kind of fear which is synonymous with being afraid. "It means a sense of awe and reverence for God and his will. It means that in deciding on the great adventure of marriage, you are not reckoning without God."[1] This involves the acceptance of marriage for what it is in God's purpose according to the definition we have already given: the life-long union of one man with one woman to the exclusion of all others. But it means too that there is a humble belief that God has guided us to this step, and that the marriage is according to his will. Where there is a strong sense of fulfilling the purpose of God, and marriage is accepted as a vocation, there is a basis of happiness which nothing can destroy.

[1] Parsons, op. cit., p. 26.

It will be found in practice that many couples are glad of the reassurance which a talk along these lines brings them. Some may raise questions and express doubts. Others will reveal that they definitely need help in rising to the Christian ideals of marriage. We cannot force it on them, but the opportunity of pointing the way will come later.

11

The Threefold Plan

The second half of the Introduction gives the three reasons why God ordained marriage. They are (*a*) the establishing of families, (*b*) the hallowing of the sex instinct, and (*c*) companionship and mutual help. They are all of equal importance, and we must certainly be prepared to discuss each in turn. On these subjects guidance is expected more than on any other.

THE FAMILY

The 1928 service, which has been in common use for many years and in a slightly revised form is now one of the two official forms, has improved on the wording of 1662: "It was ordained for the increase of mankind according to the will of God". This is still further improved in the Church of Ireland Prayer Book by the addition of the words "and for the due ordering of families and households". The will of God is not simply the procreation of children, but that as children are born into the world they should come as members of a family, with parents who have taken one another with life-long vows of fidelity and love, and a home which cannot be broken. This is every child's birthright. In the atmosphere of stability which such a home provides, children can be "brought up in the fear and nurture of the Lord, and to the praise of his holy Name".

We have to try to show the great privilege and responsibility of founding a family. First we should make sure that the couple have talked over together the question of having children. They nearly always have, and in almost every case they say they want to have children. Some have even decided how many. But in the vast majority of cases nowadays there is a qualification: *not yet*. And so before you have a chance of talking about bringing up a family you are right into the subject of family planning. What guidance have we to offer here?

First, I think we should start from the point of the desire eventually to have a family. This must never be lost sight of. If there is to be some form of contraception in the first months or years of marriage, it must be as much for the sake of the children who are to come as it is for the sake of the parents. Selfishness in every form is very wrong, and to avoid parenthood for entirely selfish reasons cannot be tolerated.

There are often good reasons why the conception of a child should be delayed. They may be financial, or to do with accommodation, or there may be simply the desire to become adjusted to one another in the new relationship before the arrival of a third party. It is impossible to say that any one of these is right or wrong in a given instance. I would venture the opinion that far too many couples exaggerate the economic motive, and might be happier if they accepted a baby as soon as nature could send one, even if it meant doing without some of the "necessities" which only a short time ago were "luxuries". And I wonder if anything can help husband and wife to become adjusted to each other so quickly as the expectation of their first child.

This is merely an opinion, not a dogmatic statement. What can be said with certainty is that, whether or not a couple practises contraception in the beginning of marriage, many will do so at some point in their married life. Christian opinion, apart from the Roman Catholic Church, has come to accept scientific methods of birth control as morally neutral and a part of modern life. The old argument that they are "unnatural" carries little weight, for the same can be said of many other things which a doctor may prescribe. All surgery, for example, is strictly speaking unnatural, as are such aids to better living as spectacles and false teeth. Scientific contraception is neither morally wrong nor morally right in itself. If used for selfish ends, it is clearly wrong. If used to enable a couple to fulfil the proper function of marriage according to their vow to live together after God's ordinance, even when the conception of a child is not desirable, it can be wholly good.

In point of fact every couple uses some kind of birth control. Complete abstinence is one way, and no Christian would wish to deny that where it is really necessary the grace of God will be given to make it possible. But of all "methods" this would seem to be the most "unnatural". It certainly puts a great strain on the couple and the risk of a marriage coming to grief in these circumstances is considerable. The New Testament is not on the side of complete abstinence. St Paul in 1 Corinthians 7.5 is clear: "Do not cheat each other of normal sexual intercourse, unless of course you both decide to abstain temporarily to make special opportunity for fasting and prayer. But afterwards you should resume relations as before, or you will expose yourselves to the obvious temptation of the devil" (J. B. Phillips' translation). Notice that the motive for this *temporary* abstinence is not contraceptive. There can be a spiritual reason for abstaining from intercourse, as there is for fasting from food, but there is nothing spiritual in abstaining simply to avoid conception.

A modification of abstinence is the so-called "safe period". It is not entirely "safe", and in a case where a pregnancy was absolutely forbidden on medical grounds it would be folly to rely on it. For many it is difficult to calculate as it involves reckoning backwards from an uncertain date, and a good deal of margin has to be left for errors in calculation. Moreover, the element of mathematical reckoning is not entirely consistent with that degree of spontaneity which is desirable in married love. It is all a bit artificial, in fact unnatural. All the same, if we have to deal with a couple who are uneasy about other methods, we may tell them that they should consult a doctor about the safe period.

It is in fact best that we should in every case direct those who want to know about family planning to the experts in this field. This may be their own doctor, or it may be one of the Clinics run by the Family Planning Association. There is usually close co-operation between the F.P.A. and the Marriage Guidance Council, and I have found it useful to be in touch with both. A couple fixing up an appointment at the Clinic should mention the name of the clergyman who recommended them as this confirms their *bona fides*. It is a part of our own efficiency to know where our own province ends and to call in the service of others. We can advise on the moral and spiritual aspects of birth control but not on technical details. There are doctors who recognize their limitations in dealing with a patient whose basic problems are spiritual, and call on the help of a clergyman. We should willingly return the compliment.

Part of our guidance to a couple who want to postpone the arrival of a first child is to advise them to go where they will get the best advice. It is not satisfactory in this most important matter for them to rely on the imperfect knowledge of well-meaning friends or articles in popular magazines. It is still worse for them to practise *coitus interruptus* which from every point of view is indefensible. This is something *we* can say to them without any fear of contradiction by a doctor. As Anne Proctor says:

It is bad both for husband and wife, particularly the latter. Many women who suffer from nerves and sleeplessness owe their troubles to this method of frustrating each other in marriage. It is the antithesis of the attitude of *giving*; it is neither good nor reliable, and it is a starting point for resentment of every kind.[1]

[1] Proctor, op. cit., p. 65.

There are other things that need to be said to a young couple on this subject. It ought to be obvious that the decision about when and when not to use contraceptives must be a joint one in which husband and wife are in complete agreement. And they should both be convinced, not only that it is expedient, but that it is right. If a thing is right, then it is a mistake to regard it as a second best. This really is a very important point, for doubts and fears and scruples can wreck a marriage. There are certainly many cases where it is the only right thing to do to make use of contraceptives. In many instances this may be true of the first months of marriage. I still feel that there are probably too many couples putting off their first baby, and that we should certainly warn against delaying for too long.

For one thing, as long as contraceptives are used, there is no way of knowing that the couple will be capable of having children at all. When this is found out, it is possible to consult a Family Planning Clinic, which of course is just as much interested in helping couples to *have* children when they want them as in preventing them when they do not want them. But if advice of this kind is needed, the sooner it is sought the better. An even more important reason for not delaying the founding of a family for too long, is the priceless contribution that children make to a marriage and a home. If a couple get used to living without children, it can happen that they develop a joint selfishness which will not provide the best atmosphere into which babies will eventually come.

Important as the subject of family planning is, the most important thing to set before a couple preparing for marriage is the joy and responsibility of bringing up children for God. This can be discussed here, or later when the prayer for the gift of children is being studied. The latter is to be recommended, as the discussion on family planning has inevitably stressed that the desire to have children is not the only reason for physical intercourse, and that married love has a purpose of its own quite apart from the begetting of children. So we

pass naturally to the second part of the threefold purpose of
marriage.

SEX

Not many people will wish to retain the wording of the 1662
service when it comes to the second reason why God ordained
Holy Matrimony. Once when I was asked to take a wedding
at a church where the 1662 Prayer Book was strictly adhered
to in (almost) everything, I was told by the vicar that he
usually "left out the awkward bits"! The reference to sin, and
the avoidance of fornication, may be all right, though I think
the Irish Prayer Book puts it better: "for the hallowing of the
union betwixt man and woman, and for the avoidance of
sin". But the implication of the latter half of the sentence in
the 1662 service is that marriage is a concession to "such
persons as have not the gift of continency". The intention
may have been right: to stress that there were two ways,
sexually speaking, of keeping oneself an undefiled member
of Christ's body, either by living chastely in matrimony (as
the 1549 service put it) or by remaining continent if unmarried. But the impression given is unfortunate and savours of
Manichaeism rather than the New Testament. *The Oxford
Dictionary of the Christian Church* says: "The 'avoidance of
sin', though founded on Scripture (1 Cor. 7.2,9), derives
chiefly from the teaching of St Augustine, who concentrated
on the negative aspects of the union and did not see in matrimony a means of grace."[1] Unfortunately St Augustine, whose
immoral life before his conversion coloured his subsequent
attitudes, was followed in this respect by many others who
taught celibacy as a higher way of life.

The 1928 service approaches the subject from a totally
different angle. It is wholly positive. "Secondly, it was
ordained in order that the natural instincts and affections,

[1] Article on "Matrimony".

implanted by God, should be hallowed and directed aright: that those who are called by God to this holy estate should continue therein in pureness of living." This is an improvement even on the 1927 suggestion which ran: "that those who are not called by God to remain unmarried, but are by Him led to this holy estate, should continue...". In the grand affirmation, "called by God to this holy estate", there is no negative suggestion whatever.

This is what we have got to get across to the couples we prepare for marriage. We are to let them know that Christians believe that the natural instincts and affections are implanted by God. It is an insult to God who made us that way to believe anything else. Therefore sex is something to be gladly accepted as one of God's gifts which he has given us *richly to enjoy*. In spite of the apparent emancipation of young people to-day there are still many who have inhibitions about sex. It is part of our job to put them on the right track. Leslie Tizard describes sexual intercourse as

> a way by which two lovers, trying to reach complete companionship, are helped towards it. If they don't achieve sexual harmony because of inhibitions in one or both of them, or because their knowledge or technique are faulty, their progress towards a perfectly satisfying life together may be seriously retarded. For the more they love each other the more they will feel the need of the complete and mutual expression which nature has made possible through sex. If they do not achieve it, irritation and nervous strain may undermine the life of companionship they are trying to build up together.[1]

Most of what I have learned about the work of the Ministry has come from experience rather than lectures or books. This is sometimes called learning the hard way, and an illustration will show the truth of the description. I married a nice young couple whom I thought reasonably well prepared for the step they were taking. I had given them a fair amount of time

---

[1] *Guide to Marriage*, Allen & Unwin. The whole chapter on "Getting a sound attitude to sex" is admirable.

and been through all the aspects of marriage with them. Over a year later they came back to see me—separately. The marriage was breaking up, for the elementary reason that one of the parties had never really accepted the physical implications. I fear I was not able to do much to help at that stage. But I learned then that it is fatal to take anything for granted. We ought to make quite sure that those we marry are accepting marriage in its totality, and that as far as possible they are free from fears and inhibitions. I say "as far as possible" because there is a natural shyness and reticence which cannot really be broken down till after marriage. This is no bad thing. There is still a place for modesty.

Respect for the shyness of those who feel that the intimate side of marriage is something too personal and sacred to discuss with others leads me to believe that there are better ways of dealing with the subject. Of course if we are specifically asked to speak about sex relations, we should not shrink from doing so. But experience suggests that most couples prefer it otherwise. It is interesting that Canon Hugh Warner, who wrote and spoke so beautifully on the subject, thought it best that the vicar should not come to be known as the person who "does that kind of thing". The Marriage Guidance Council courses devote one evening to the physical side, and no doubt frank discussion in a group of that kind can be carried on in a happy atmosphere free from any kind of embarrassment. Sometimes a couple likes to be told by a doctor the things they ought to know, and that could be combined with advice about birth control and a medical check-up.

For myself, I am convinced that the best way of imparting the knowledge required is through the reading of a suitable book. There is a wide choice and we should be ready to recommend one or more. *The Threshold of Marriage* is an official publication of the Church of England and is splendid as far as it goes. Being a booklet of only 32 pages, it is the kind of thing which most parishes could afford to give away. For greater detail on the physical side I think Leslie J. Tizard's *Guide to Marriage* is unsurpassed. No-one could complain that it is difficult to read and it deals frankly and fully with all that anyone needs to know. Other well-tried books are *The Art of Marriage* by Mary Macauley, and *The Sex Factor in Marriage* by Helena Wright. Of a different kind, and definitely not a book on sex technique, I strongly recommend *Background to Marriage* by Anne Proctor. I suggest it as an addition to *Guide to Marriage* rather than as a substitute for it. For the pastor's own reading, Theodor Bovet's *A Handbook to Marriage and Marriage Guidance* is invaluable. It is in fact one of the great books.

Books can be lent, or better still stocked for sale on the church book-stall. On occasion I have had an arrangement with a local bookseller to keep a supply of whatever book I was recommending. Even in these days a young couple can be a bit shy of asking in a shop for *The Sex Factor in Marriage*. But if they ask for the book the vicar recommends, the result will be the same.

COMPANIONSHIP

The third purpose of marriage is expressed in words which (apart from the spelling) have not needed any change since 1549. "The mutual society, help, and comfort, that the one ought to have of the other, both in prosperity and adversity", is a subject which can provoke a lively discussion. This after all is the most permanent of all the joys of marriage. Children eventually grow up and go out to found homes of their own. Physical passion weakens with old age, though it still has its place. But the friendship of husband and wife remains to the end. We need to impress our young people that they must be not only parents and lovers; they must be *pals*. Is this self-evident? If it was, we should not see husbands who expect their wives to mother their children and give them all that a wife should give, while they find their chief recreation in going out with the boys; or wives who are so engrossed with their interests outside the home, or even their house and children, that they have no time to spend in just being with their husbands. In the ideal marriage, husband and wife find each other's company and conversation the most satisfying of all pleasures.

The companionship of husband and wife, however, is not meant to exclude other companionship. The happier they are in each other's company, the more they have to give to society at large. We should encourage a spirit of hospitality in the home, the continuance of old friendships as well as the making of new ones, and perhaps give a word of warning about the folly of that possessiveness which sometimes reveals itself in jealousy. In these days of emphasis on stewardship, Christian couples need to be taught to see their homes, and even their marriage, as something God has given them to use for others.

Nowadays the home may be the problem. For reasons quite beyond their control a great many people start their married life without a home of their own. We must be very sympathetic about this, knowing the difficulties involved in finding a house or a flat. But I think we should be prepared to point out the great disadvantages of having to live with parents. It will always be "till we find a place of our own", but those early months are vital for the whole marriage and I have seen the mischief that can result from two generations living together. We must not sound too alarming in giving this warning, and there may be cases where the relationship works out very well. But as a matter of general principle we can press, I think, for a literal interpretation of the words, "For this reason a man shall *leave* his father and mother and be joined to his wife".

Not only living with parents or in-laws, but any accommodation which does not give full independence—kitchen, bathroom, and all—is very much of a second best. If the two are to become one, they need a place of their own in which to grow together. This becomes even more important when the family begins to arrive. Lack of accommodation, as we have seen, is a major reason why people put off having children.

Another is insufficient money, and this is one of the reasons why almost all girls continue to work after they are married. Today any girl who, on getting married, gives up her job in order to become a full-time housewife is bound to be the odd one out among her friends. This is the social pattern which has developed and we must come to terms with it. It may be a good thing, and is certainly the practice even where the money is not a primary consideration. But it does make the companionship side of marriage slightly more difficult to achieve.

What we have to encourage is the development of a real home. This is the place where both the man and the woman find the mutual society, help, and comfort which they need in order to face the demands of life. In the ideal family it is a home built around the worship of God. Its happiness does not depend on the number and size of its rooms, or the lavishness of its furniture, but on two people who know that they are "joint heirs of the grace of life". This mutual support will carry a couple through hard times as well as sunny days, for it is there "both in prosperity and adversity".

Perhaps it is fitting to end this section on companionship by stressing its importance in the life of the clergyman and his wife. Possibly lay people envy us the amount of time we spend at home, and imagine that we see more of our wives than most men do. The opposite is often the case. The vicarage is our study, our office, and our consulting room. Except at meal-times we are seldom away from our work during the day, and in the evening, when others relax, we have meetings, interviews, and suchlike to fit in. It is a great life and we would not change it for worlds. But if we are not careful, our wives suffer for it. It is not a particularly Christian act to offer the fag-end of our life to the woman we promised to love, comfort, honour, and keep, even if the excuse is that we are busy in God's service. We must not prepare other people for their marriage and neglect our own. We ought to be busy for the greater part of the day, but some time must also be set aside as sacred to the home. And if we preach to others the value of the day of rest, we should not fail to keep the weekly day off ourselves. Keeping our marriage in a state of continuous freshness is as much our duty as any part of our ministry.

12
Marriage Vows

The Introduction ends with an appeal to the congregation that if anyone knows any impediment to the marriage they should say so at once. This, we can explain, is a kind of final calling of the banns and the likelihood of any interruption of the service at this point is very remote indeed. The same is true of the following words addressed to the couple. It is entirely right that a last appeal should be made to them to disclose any reason why they may not be lawfully married, but the chances are against there being any response. In the overwhelming majority of cases there is no impediment, and if there *were* a case of someone committing bigamy, having got so far he or she would hardly make a confession even in response to so extremely solemn a charge. I have been present at a wedding where the priest said: "I am leaving out the next section ("I require and charge you both . . .") because I know that it does not apply." This is quite inexcusable. If it became known that he did that in some cases, what would the people think of those for whom he did not omit the words?

It is just possible that when this charge is made, although there is no legal impediment, a bride or bridegroom may be overcome with panic at what is so obviously a point of no return. It is our task for the most part to reassure; but if we have reason to believe that there are serious doubts or problems, it is at this point at the interview that we can deal with them. There are undoubtedly people whose marriages have been unhappy from the start who wish that the clergyman had had the insight and the courage to challenge them plainly about the advisability of going forward. The matter is important, and we shall return to some of the problem cases in a later chapter.

"If no impediment be alleged, then shall the Priest say unto the man", reads the rubric, and we assume that no impediment will be alleged. What follows is known as the Espousals. It may be of interest to the couple to know something about the origin and history of the ceremony which was "a formal and religious recognition of what is now termed an engagement, and took place sometimes months, sometimes years, before the marriage itself".[1] In the Sarum Manual it took place when the couple were still at the door of the church. The important thing to emphasize is that before the marriage can proceed there must be a formal declaration by both parties of their willingness. No marriage can take place against the will of either partner. If consent has not been given, the marriage is legally void. For this reason it is essential that the response "I will" should be audible.

It is equally important to point out the nature of the question to which they are to say "I will". They are words of unselfish love and total commitment. There is acceptance of marriage in its totality, "to live together according to God's law" (or "after God's ordinance", 1662). There is the promise to love, comfort, honour, and keep her in every circumstance, "in sickness and in health". And this is to be in a union which by its very nature must be exclusive and permanent.

If this is true, why, it may be asked, is it necessary to make a vow about it? If there is real love, it will be both lasting and monogamous. Why introduce the element of law which tends to vitiate the quality of love? But the two are no more incompatible than the now famous charity and chastity which are each supposed by some to exclude the other. It is not "either—or", but "both—and". On the essential nature of

---

[1] *The Tutorial Prayer Book*, Neil & Willoughby, The Harrison Trust, 1912.

marriage vows I venture to quote what I have said to the young couples themselves:

> After the promise to love, comfort, honour and keep, in sickness and in health, it may seem an anti-climax to have added the words "forsaking all other, keep thee only unto her". How could anyone so deeply committed even think of not keeping only to her? Yet experience shows how wise it is to have these words, so unmistakable in their meaning, embedded in the marriage service. Human nature is weak. The temptations of the flesh are strong. You do not think infidelity could ever be possible now, but you do not know what you may feel about it in ten years' time. The day may come when every other motive will fail you and you will be driven back to this fundamental fact: "I have made a vow; and to that vow, by the grace of God, I remain true." That vow is not "till we get tired of one another", or "till one of us meets someone else more satisfying", but "so long as ye both shall live".[1]

It is, of course, when a married couple takes seriously the binding nature of their vows that they are determined to make their marriage succeed, and find increasing happiness as a result.

The question to the woman in the 1928 Prayer Book, which is the first of the alternative questions in the experimental form of 1966, is identical with that addressed to the man. The second of the alternatives in the 1966 service is in the same form as in the Prayer Book of 1662, containing the question "Wilt thou obey him and serve him?" The omission of "obey" in 1928 was in order to safeguard against misunderstanding. An utterly selfish husband might insist on anything he liked and expect compliance because his wife had promised to obey him. But this is a complete travesty of the situation and ignores the content of the vows as a whole. The man has already vowed to love his wife, to comfort, honour, and keep her. The woman's vow is made in the light of this. She accepts him at his word and promises to stay with him, serving his needs in her own particular way, and recognizing him as the

[1] Parsons, op. cit., pp. 64, 65.

head of the household. He is this in law. He gives his name, his protection, and his support. A woman need not be regarded as inferior or less emancipated because she thankfully accepts her position, which is one of very great dignity, and recognizes that her husband has the ultimate responsibility.

After the Espousals, when both parties have said "I will", follows the not unimportant ceremony of giving away. It is well to give clear instructions about how we like this to be done. To the question "Who giveth this woman to be married to this man?" there is no answer in words. The best way of symbolizing what is happening is for the father of the bride to take her right hand and present her to the priest, who will then take her hand and join it to the bridegroom's right hand. In this way we show, not only that the girl's parents are giving her away, but that she is definitely leaving the old home to form a new relationship; and also that the parents, represented by the father (the head of the family—see previous paragraph), are giving up their daughter to God, in order that God, through his Church and Minister, may bestow her upon the husband of her choice. This is an important principle, and the ritual should make it clear.

As bride and bridegroom stand with their right hands joined, the man repeats, phrase by phrase, the words of betrothal. We should tell them exactly how we want them to stand—turning slightly towards each other perhaps, so that the words, which are addressed to the bride, are spoken *to* her, and not to the clergyman. We may like to suggest just how their hands should be joined, in a firm grip like a handshake rather than in a dilettante fashion. And we should tell them precisely how much of the words we shall give each time before pausing for them to repeat what we say. Experience teaches that the shorter the section the less likely are they to make any mistake. We need scarcely stop to expound every phrase, since we have covered the ground in explaining the Espousals. It may be well, however, to interpret the word "troth", connected as it is with truth. To plight one's troth is to pledge one's true word, or loyalty.

The ritual of loosing hands and the woman with her right hand taking the man by his right hand needs to be explained. In practice it really means loosing hands and joining them up again. The words spoken by the woman, as we have noted, may include "and to obey" without any fear of compromising her position. It has to be admitted that this may not always have been the case. In the Sarum Manual on which the vows are based there was no "to love and to cherish" in the man's words, and the woman promised "to be bonere and buxum in bedde and at the borde". "Faithful" and "obedient" are true translations of the two old words.

The joining and loosing of hands and the saying of the words may well be gone through in detail if there is a rehearsal, and the same is true of the ceremony of the ring. The rubric directs that the man shall give the woman a ring, laying the same upon the book. By custom the best man produces the ring and puts it on the book, but this is not strictly correct. He should give it to the bridegroom who himself places it on the book. We may see in this action the symbolic surrender of himself to God, in much the same way as the bride was given up to God. The priest gives the ring back to the man to place on the fourth finger of the woman's left hand. In providing an optional prayer for the blessing of the ring the 1966 service is recognizing what has already become a common practice.

As late as 1549 the man was directed to give the woman not only a ring but "other tokens of spousage, as gold or silver, laying the same upon the book". In 1552 this was omitted and "with the accustomed duty to the Priest and Clerk" was substituted. This was an unfortunate change, and though it persists in the 1662 rubric I doubt if the fees are ever paid in this way nowadays. Both the 1928 service and the 1966 experimental service omit the reference to the accustomed duty, but do not restore the gift of gold or silver. What these were intended to symbolize is contained in the words "and all my worldly goods with thee I share". Some may regret the passing of the words "with all my worldly goods I thee endow". The wedding ring, being of gold or platinum, is a sufficient visible token of the man's promise to support his wife. "With my body I thee worship" is a promise of service with all a man's physical powers, not just a reference to love-making. "Honour" instead of "worship" is perhaps an improvement.

If it is desired to say something to a couple about the economic side of marriage, the reference to "all my worldly goods" gives the opportunity. Here we need to be delicate in our approach as some couples may be as reticent about talking of finance as they are about sex, perhaps even more so. Nevertheless, we can try to show the importance of living within our means, of husband and wife being open about money matters, and of saving something for the future. We may also feel it right to recommend life insurance, and we certainly should put the Christian point of view on the stewardship of all our possessions and the need for systematic and proportional giving. But the main point at the moment is the obligation of the husband to provide for his wife. Although in most cases the wife will also be earning at the start, the time will come when the arrival of a family makes this no longer possible. I have said that some couples are shy about speaking of their financial affairs. Others are only too glad to find someone to talk to who is ready to show an interest and to help with advice. In *Guide to Marriage*, which I have recommended as being excellent on the sex side of marriage, Leslie Tizard devotes four of his short chapters to finance, hire-purchase, and house and furniture. These things do matter very much.

After the ring has been placed on the bride's finger, the couple will kneel. The people remain standing, and the omission of the words "Let us pray", as in the 1928 service, helps to avoid any confusion about this. A whispered direction to the bride and bridegroom to kneel down is all that is required. All these matters should be made clear at the interview, and again at the rehearsal. The prayer which follows is a gem and contains enough theology to be the basis of a complete treatise on marriage. The reference to Isaac and Rebecca is left out in the new service and the omission is no great loss. It was introduced from a prayer in the Sarum Manual at the blessing of the ring, in which mention was made of "bracelets and jewels of gold given of the one to the other for tokens of their matrimony". We may wonder whether Isaac and Rebecca were an ideal couple in view of the events described in Genesis 27. But at least there is no record of polygamy in their story. From the didactic point of view the prayer emphasizes the connection between keeping the vows and remaining in perfect love and peace together. And this is made possible by the blessing of God.

While the couple are still on their knees the priest will once again join their right hands. It may be necessary to explain that when he stoops to do this he is not indicating that they are to stand up. The joining of hands and the words which accompany it should be most solemnly performed as the climax of the service. The declaration which follows should be equally solemnly pronounced. The sense of awe which comes over a couple when they hear that they are now man and wife together should give place to calm assurance and trust as they receive the blessing. The Minister can convey something of this contrast in his manner and voice. If bride and bridegroom are really open to receive what God so freely gives, they can be assured of grace to live the new life together to which they have now voluntarily and whole-heartedly committed themselves. As we proceed with our explanation of the second part of the service we find all the material we need to bring home to them the spiritual resources which are available.

13

The Blessing of the Marriage

The 1662 Prayer Book had no sub-headings in the Form of Solemnization of Matrimony. The 1928 form helpfully introduced sub-titles—the Introduction, the Marriage, the Benediction. The latest form of the service has changed the last to the Blessing of the Marriage, surely a further improvement. The rubric which introduces this part of the service leaves the choice of the Psalm open, while recommending Psalms 128, 67, or 37.3–7 as suitable. As already noted, a hymn is often sung in place of a Psalm, a concession to those who find difficulty over the pointing, but the more correct way of overcoming this problem is for the Psalm to be said. If the procession of "the Priest, followed by the man and the woman" seems to require music, there is no reason why there should not be a few bars of organ music while they "go to the Lord's Table", and the Psalm be said when they arrive there.

We have reached the point in the interview where we can broach the subject of definite Christian commitment and life in the Church. It has indeed been implicit in much of what has been said already, but now it becomes the main subject of the talk. Here is the moment at which we become more conscious than ever of the differences in spiritual experience of those we interview. Some will be committed Christian people, faithful and regular communicants. This makes it very easy to turn to the subject of a shared faith, which is the only sure basis for marriage. "So you see, we have pronounced you to be man and wife together, and you have received the blessing. Now, as your first action as Mr and Mrs Jones, you are going to walk together, as the rubric tells you, to the Lord's Table. This is something which is going to mean a lot to you. Again and again you have knelt here to receive the Holy Communion. And now on your wedding day you are coming to that same sacred spot while you and all the congregation join in prayer." The symbolism of kneeling at the Communion rail is significant whether there is to be Holy Communion at the wedding or not.

What can we say to those who are lapsed communicants, or who have never been confirmed, or perhaps are scarcely even church-goers in any shape or form? I have already suggested that we should not repel those who seek marriage in church, but try to draw them in. The approach in such cases could be something like this: "I know you are not communicants, and so the symbolism of this part of the service might mean less to you than it would to some others. For you are moving forward to kneel at the place where we come to receive the Holy Communion. All the same, I think the meaning need not be entirely lost. The first part of the service has taken place at the chancel step. You were standing quite near the congregation when you took your vows. Now you leave your relations and friends and set out on your own. And at the end of that first walk together, you kneel side by side to pray. I believe you will find that that is just what you want to do at that particular moment. You have taken a tremendous step. You want to seek God's blessing in prayer."

We shall see to it that a Prayer Book is in place so that we can hand it to them, open at the pages, when we begin the prayers. This time the people all kneel, "the man and the woman kneeling before the Lord's Table, the Priest standing at the Table, and turning his face towards them". In our explanation we can, if we think it appropriate, point out the significance of the Lesser Litany as an invocation of the Holy Trinity to help us to pray, and of the Lord's Prayer as the model for all our praying. Each versicle and response is taken from the Psalms (86.2; 20.1,2; 61.3; and 102.1) and I find it particularly profitable to stress the first. "O Lord, save thy servant, and thy handmaid" is a specific prayer for the bride and bridegroom that they may know the saving power of God. And they are to respond in words which are less a prayer than an affirmation, "Who put their trust in thee".

Sooner or later we have got to challenge the couple on the subject of a vital faith, and this may be as good a point as any. Are they putting their trust in God, and do they really want him to save his "servant" and his "handmaid"? Are they in fact his servants in any deep sense at all? Canon Bryan Green suggests a quite direct approach:

> You say you want God to bless your wedding; why should He bless you at all? You haven't bothered very much about Him, have you? Therefore why should He bother about you?[1]

Before we dismiss this as being too blunt we need to ask ourselves whether our motive for doing so is not cowardice, or a desire to remain vague on the subject of conversion. Canon Green goes on:

> Our business is to try and show that though God in His love is ever ready to meet us when we turn to Him, yet in the lives of those with whom we are speaking, again and again what is wrong is that they are unconverted. God is of no real importance in their lives. They are quite certainly not "alive to God through Jesus Christ". Here we must be fearless and honest, uncompromising with the truth of the Gospel. We shall not try and browbeat those who have given us the privilege of talking with them. We certainly must not be dogmatic or domineering, but we can be plain, straightforward and kindly.

Plain, straightforward, and kindly is an excellent description of what should be our manner of approach as we set before the couple the claims of the gospel. Where they are in any way responsive, the first of the three prayers in this section contains the teaching we can use to point the way to faith. It asks, not only for a blessing, but in a specific request prays that God will sow the seed of eternal life in their hearts. We

[1] *The Practice of Evangelism*, Hodder & Stoughton, p. 74.

can show that this is a prayer for nothing less than that they may know God, and Jesus Christ whom he has sent (John 17.3). This new life is pledged in Baptism, but needs to be consciously accepted and appropriated. God's offer of new life in Christ calls for a response of total commitment. As we see those we are speaking to are taking in the message, we can gauge how much or how little we need to tell them of the facts of the Gospel. We need to remember that there is great ignorance of the New Testament, and we need to be very simple in our explanation of the way to forgiveness and newness of life. Yet in the end salvation does not depend on a knowledge of theology but on knowing Christ. We have to bring people to a point of decision for him.

In the case of those who have not been confirmed this is the point at which to suggest that they should attend classes. Here is one reason for starting marriage preparation in good time, so that Confirmation can be arranged before the wedding if at all possible. I think we ought to be prepared to instruct such inquiries for Confirmation at any time, without waiting for our next series of official classes. If one of the parties is already confirmed, he or she should be asked to come with the other as to a refresher course. If both are confirmed but lapsed, we may suggest their joining any form of adult instruction course which we run in the parish, as well as renewing their church attendance and communicant life. But even then we shall not make the mistake of thinking that head knowledge and regularity in religious duties are always to be equated with heart conversion and a personal knowledge of our Lord.

We shall of course have the joy of preparing sincerely Christian couples for marriage as well as those who are on the fringe. The prayer that God may sow the seed of eternal life in their hearts is not redundant for them, even though they have already begun the spiritual life. There is no one who does not need to advance in the life abundant, in other words to know God better. The first step of faith and surrender is the start of a life of devotion and obedience. The prayer goes on to ask "that whatsoever in thy holy Word they shall profitably learn, they may in deed fulfil the same". The Prayer Book expects a standard of devotional life which many church-people fail to follow. Obedience to God's Word presupposes at least regular devotional reading of the Bible as well as attendance at church where it is expounded. We should take the opportunity of discussing with those we are preparing the whole subject of the devotional life, and to what extent their prayers and Bible reading will be a shared experience.[1] As they are to be no longer two but one, it may be expected that their life at the deepest level, their fellowship with God, will find expression in joint, as well as individual, prayer. And incidentally, if they abide in God's love unto their lives' end, there is not much fear for the lasting quality of their love for each other.

The prayer for the heritage and gift of children is to be omitted when the woman is past child-bearing. Occasionally a younger couple will mention that they know from their doctor that they will not be able to have children, and ask that this prayer be omitted. For the rest, we have the age of the bride on the banns form and we can be guided by that. In cases where we are in real difficulty we can ask tactfully. It is better to include the prayer in doubtful cases than to omit it and cause offence. But if we have established a relationship of confidence, the matter will probably have been settled at an early stage of the interview.

The prayer is not only for children, it is that they may see their children Christianly and virtuously brought up to the praise and honour of God. We have left behind in the earlier part of the preparation the question of family planning, the size and spacing of the family to be planned, and so on. Here

---

[1] A useful little book to give in this connection is *In Wonder, Love, and Praise*, a book of prayers and readings for husband and wife, by David J. Farmbrough, S.P.C.K., 1966, price 3s. 6d.

our preoccupation is with the bringing up of the children as Christians. We should emphasize the place of prayer in all the other preparations for the arrival of an infant. Undoubtedly the love and joy and peace of the home is the biggest factor in influencing the children. We can speak of Baptism, of what the Church will do to help through cradle-roll and *crèche*, Sunday School, Young Wives' Groups, and Mothers' Union (with its excellent helps in the teaching of children), and of the Church of England Men's Society for the fathers. But when all is said, we must insist that there is absolutely no substitute for the Christian home. We do not need to go into great detail about the training of children at this stage, but we should say enough to fire the imagination with the thought of the immense privilege of co-operating with God in the creation of new lives, and of bringing up those entrusted to us to be members of Christ, children of God, and inheritors of the Kingdom of Heaven.

The third prayer is abbreviated and simplified in the 1928 version, and even so is the longest prayer in the service. For all its antiquated language—"betwixt", "amiable", "matrons" —it is a prayer of singular beauty and is basically a petition for true love. Marriage is the symbol of the unity between Christ and the Church. The love of Christ was revealed in his giving himself for his bride. That is the kind of love for which we pray in this prayer. It is the love of utter devotion which desires above everything else the highest well-being of the loved one. As we expound this standard we can show once again that it is impossible to attain apart from the grace of God. Human love can only reach these heights when it is in fact the love of God shed abroad in our hearts by the Holy Spirit.

On this note we may well end the interview, simply reading the final blessing without comment. We can then fix the date of the rehearsal, if this has not been done, and at that occasion we can explain the details of going into the vestry to sign the register. It should be a natural thing to close the interview with a prayer. To kneel may be a trifle embarrassing, while to remain seated is rather slovenly. The obvious solution is to stand. The prayer should be quite simple, commending John and Mary by name to the care of God.

14

Taking The Service

ATTENTION TO DETAIL

In using the Prayer Book service as the basis of our talk with
the couple we have already commented on a number of points
connected with the taking of the wedding. There remain a
few matters that are worth mentioning, for no detail is unimportant, and nothing should be left to chance.

The priest should be at the church well before the bridegroom and best man are due to arrive and should be already
in his cassock to welcome them to the vestry. This, we have
already suggested at the interview, should be a quarter of an
hour before the time of the wedding. In the vestry the entries
in the register, and the certificate, should be checked. They
have probably been filled in the day before, but strictly
speaking no register should be written up until it is quite
certain that another wedding will not take place in the
church on an earlier day. If the registers were filled in a week
before, for instance, and then a couple turned up for a marriage by licence at short notice, the entry would have to be
cancelled and rewritten in the proper chronological order.

The few minutes with the bridegroom in the vestry are
important. He may need to be put at his ease, and our own
confidence and efficiency can help to steady his nerves. Vestries
are often drab and sometimes untidy. This should be
remedied as far as possible, and clean blotting paper, a table
cleared of everything except the registers, pens and ink, and
a vase of flowers can help to show that the occasion is one

which we are treating with respect. There ought to be a mirror, and the provision of a clothes-brush, shoe-brush, and hair-brush and comb would be an extra attention not un-appreciated. To ask that every vestry should have toilet and washing facilities is perhaps unrealistic, but it ought to be a goal for the future. Besides checking the registers and sprucing himself up, the bridegroom—or more probably the best man—will pay the fees if this has not been done before. Any last minute instructions should be in the nature of words of reassurance. Not "Do you remember all you have got to do?" but "Don't worry about what you have to do or say; I shall guide you at each point, and it can't go wrong."

Bridegroom and best man go to their seats at about five minutes before the time. It is good manners to conduct them there and, if there has been no rehearsal, to point out the exact spot where they are to stand. The priest will return to the vestry to robe. Here perhaps it is worth saying what ought to be obvious, that in every detail of robes and personal grooming the officiating minister must be immaculate. This is true of any and every service, but it has an added import-ance at a wedding when everyone is dressed up in honour of the occasion. Not only is it important to be well turned out, but the manner in which the clergyman takes the service is vital. Dignity is of the essence, but this is not to be confused with pomposity. The voice should be natural, neither over-dramatic nor studiedly casual. We can be intimate without being "matey", or still worse facetious. There should be an assured happiness and at the same time a solemnity which befits a great occasion.

If the priest meets the bride at the door, which is regarded by some as a mark of respect and good manners, he can have a word with the bridesmaids, and also with the bride's father, who is sometimes the most nervous person in the church. The procession should be slow and dignified. Many priests prefer to stand at the chancel steps and await the bride. Care should be taken that the bridegroom knows that he is to take up his

7

place at the chancel step when the Wedding March begins. He should be asked not to turn round and watch the bride arriving, but to incline towards her as she draws level with him, and give her a welcoming smile. Then when the bride has given her bouquet to a bridesmaid we are ready to begin the service. It is a good idea to invite the congregation, in a few carefully phrased sentences, to take their full part in the service, and especially to join in the singing and responses, and to say Amen to the prayers.

The conduct of the service will vary in slight detail in different churches, but the following extract from instructions issued by a London vicar for the guidance of his assistant clergy may suggest ways in which we can increase the orderliness of the service. After dealing with preliminary matters under five headings the paper continues:

6. When the organ voluntary stops (*a*) give out a notice encouraging all present to take part in the Service, especially hymns and responses. Explain that page numbers will be given "in case you have not already found the place"; (*b*) announce first the hymn—number "in the green book"; then the first line and then repeat number.

7. After the hymn announce, "The marriage service will be found on page 301 in the red books."

8. Before asking the question "N. wilt thou have this woman . . ." point at the bridegroom, and say, "Be ready to say 'I will'." This need not be repeated to the woman.

9. Turn to the bride's father and ask, "Who giveth this woman . . .?" Ensure that he hands her *right* hand to you. Take her by the right wrist and hand her to the bridegroom, saying, "Take her right hand in your right hand and say these words after me." Then say, "Release your hands." Then to the woman, "Take his *same* hand in your *same* hand and say these words after me."

10. Look hard at the best man. Hold out the book on which he will put the ring. Pick it up, give it to the man and say, "Take this ring (pause) put it on the fourth finger of her left hand, and say these words after me, 'With this ring. . . .'"

11. Say "The congregation will remain standing with heads bowed for prayer." (Then to the couple, quietly) "You two kneel down."

12. Read next prayer, then bend down and say quietly to the couple, "Remain kneeling and join your right hands together again." Then clasp their hands and say slowly, "Those whom God hath joined together. . . ."

13. After the Blessing, announce Psalm 67, giving the page number in red books (page 306), and emphasize that all should say this together, then while they are finding the place say to the couple (now standing), "When I turn round, follow me."

14. Turn and walk to the Sanctuary when Psalm is well going.[1]

We need not go any further. These instructions are not here reproduced in order to be strictly followed in every church. Any experienced parish priest will say at once that there are certain things he does differently and that he prefers his own way. But the point is that here is an example of doing all things decently and in order, in a way which obviously suits that particular parish. We shall all work out our own method, but should learn from such a carefully thought-out document the need for meticulous care in every detail.

THE ADDRESS

If there be no Communion, here shall follow the Sermon; or there shall be read some portion of Scripture. This rubric in the Alternative Service dispenses with the obligation of an address of some kind—sermon or reading of Scripture—provided there is to be Holy Communion. For one reason or another the number of weddings at which there is a Communion is not very large, so in the majority of cases an address is called for. The homily printed at the end of the 1662 Service is a catena of New Testament passages on the duties of husband and wife. It is, to say the least, strong meat for an

[1] The Reverend Norman H. Bainbridge, formerly vicar of St James', Muswell Hill. Quoted with his permission.

occasion which calls for something lighter and more digestible. Any passage of Scripture is now permitted, and 1 Corinthians 13 is often used. But "the Sermon" is clearly intended to be the first choice. Anyone who takes a wedding service without either giving an address or reading a passage of Scripture is both disregarding the Church's directive and missing a big opportunity.

That the sermon is not intended to be a private talk to the couple is clear from the 1662 homily which begins, "All ye that are married, or that intend to take the holy estate of Matrimony upon you". We shall certainly include a word to the bride and bridegroom, but not to the exclusion of the message to the congregation. Many who come to a wedding will not be in church again until the next similar occasion. We must use the opportunity to present the Christian message. But the sermon must be both short and appropriate.

It must be short because the congregation will not be in the mood for a long discourse. Five minutes is a long enough time to say something worth while. The couple can remain standing, and it is probably best for the preacher not to go into the pulpit, but to stand facing them. It would really be an advantage if the address could be given before the Psalm, when the couple are still at the chancel step and the preacher is therefore nearer to the congregation. Strict adherence to rubrical direction unfortunately rules this out. There are many possible themes for a wedding address, which basically should be a statement of the Christian view of marriage, its nature, its duties, and its resources. The great value of the address as an evangelistic weapon, which in view of the composition of so many wedding congregations it often has to be, is that in it we can show the relevance of the gospel to common life. It would be an error of judgement to preach an evangelistic sermon which had no reference to the occasion. There is no excuse for doing this when the whole subject of marriage is so closely bound up with the major themes of the gospel. Let the sermon, then, be appropriate.

Each clergyman will work out his own variations on the theme, and in the course of a long ministry in a large parish is bound to repeat himself. There is no harm in that. Some of us have heard the same Confirmation address more than once, and it need not lose its freshness through repetition. But we should have a number of different lines of approach, deciding prayerfully which is the most suitable for a particular wedding, and always being open to develop a new idea. In those parishes where there are only a few marriages each year, a brand new address might be expected for each occasion; but I am thinking of the many parishes where this would be quite impossible.

A few suggestions only are given here. It is natural to speak of love as the basis of marriage. True love must include the love of complete self-giving devotion. This is the kind of love with which God loves us and it becomes ours only as we open our lives to *his* love. This is the love of John 3.16, which can be linked with the third of the prayers in the Blessing of the Marriage.

It may be helpful to give the same message in more concrete form by making use of a biblical incident. The walk to Emmaus is a very fruitful field, whether or not we believe that the unnamed disciple with Cleopas was his wife. "Jesus himself drew near and went with them" is a subject from which to preach the ideal of Christ's companionship on the road as the couple set out together. Or the latter part of the story can be used, where Jesus is invited into the home, takes the position of host, reveals himself in the simple action of breaking bread, and withdraws himself so that they will learn to rely henceforth on his unseen presence. This story is particularly useful at Easter weddings.

There is always a danger that if we stick to simple gospel truth and apply it to the present situation we shall be accused of speaking platitudes. The accusation is more likely to come from ourselves than from those who listen to us. It is so much more gratifying to ourselves to say something rather clever. But it is the straightforward presentation of the gospel which reaches the heart. A platitude is defined as a commonplace remark, and there is nothing commonplace about the story of God's love in Christ. We need to have the courage to be simple. So we shall speak plainly about the need to build the new life on the one foundation that has been laid, and of the Lord as the builder, using the words of Psalm 127.1 as the starting-point. The wedding feast at Cana speaks of Christ as the Lord of all joy, and of obedience to him as the secret of abundant life: "Whatsoever he saith unto you, do it." There is no end to the possibilities, and the opportunity of those few minutes is enormous. Not long ago a man whom I met again after nineteen years told me that the talk I gave at his wedding brought him up with a shock and he realized he was not a Christian in any vital sense. The new start of marriage brought also a new start with God, and he and his wife had built a happy Christian home.

Style of preaching, as well as subject matter, will vary enormously with each preacher. The following sample is given, not for reproduction, but as an indication of the type of address which may be suitable for a wedding congregation which is neither deeply taught nor particularly predisposed to be receptive.

LEAD US, HEAVENLY FATHER

I am the first to be able to congratulate you on being pronounced man and wife together. All the others who have taken part with you in your wedding service will be doing so in a few minutes. Before that happens, I am going to give you a thought for the new life which you are just beginning. It is based on the hymn which you chose for the opening of the service: Lead us, Heavenly Father.

When you came to the Church today you knew that it was to be one of the most tremendous half-hours of your life. You have taken vows which commit you to live from now onwards for each other, not just for yourself. Of course you have been thinking about it for a long time, and since your engagement you have known that this is what you want to do. All the same, it is a bit awe-inspiring to make those solemn promises for better for worse, till death us do part. You stand committed, at the beginning of an unknown journey.

Something makes you feel your need of a strength greater than your own, a guiding hand upon your life more sure and steady than any other, yes, even a love greater than the love you have for each other. And so you turn to God, the Heavenly Father. You chose to begin the service with a prayer to him—

> Lead us, Heavenly Father, lead us
> O'er the world's tempestuous sea.

He always hears our prayer when we truly surrender ourselves to his guidance. The trouble is that we have often not followed his leading, we have gone our own way and got lost. There is so much in our lives which could have been better. And so we need forgiveness. It was in order that we might be forgiven that Jesus Christ came into the world, "felt its keenest woe" as your hymn puts it, and in the end gave his life as a sacrifice for our sins. He is the Saviour. We pray—

> Saviour, breathe forgiveness o'er us;
> All our weakness thou dost know.

We all of us need forgiveness, not only from God but from each other. Even in marriage this is true. If anything crops up between you—and because we can all be selfish it sometimes does—let there be immediate reconciliation, or as St Paul put it, "forgiving one another, as God in Christ forgave you".

The Heavenly Father to lead us; the Saviour to forgive us. And then in the third verse we ask God's Holy Spirit to come right into our lives and make it all real as a personal experience—

> Spirit of our God, descending,
> Fill our hearts with heavenly joy.

Joy, love, unspoiled pleasure, peace that nothing can destroy, these are the things which we want for you in your marriage. But they will not come to you automatically. It is as you open your hearts to the Holy Spirit that you can know the abundant life of love and joy and peace.

You have made these splendid vows to live each for the other. I am afraid we cannot keep those vows in our own strength. Then let the Holy Spirit come and live within you and give you *his* strength. He will lead you to Jesus the Saviour who forgives, and helps us to forgive. So you will know the Heavenly Father, and in the enjoyment of his love will love one another with that unselfish devotion which will bring you lasting happiness.

THE COMMUNION

"It is convenient that the new-married persons should receive the Holy Communion at the time of their marriage, or at the first opportunity after their marriage." This is the rubric in the 1662 Prayer Book, and there have always been some who observed it by having Communion at the time of the Marriage Service. For a variety of reasons the majority do not, and while it is very desirable that where both are communicants they should, we need to take account of the total situation before pressing them to do so. Although the couple themselves might desire it, the parents may not be entirely sympathetic. It is best to leave the choice with the bride and bridegroom, giving them every encouragement but not bringing any pressure to bear.

Commonly, when there is a celebration of Holy Communion, only the bride and bridegroom communicate. This is a great pity. It is understandable that when there is a large congregation of guests, possibly somewhat heterogeneous religiously, the invitation should not be given to all and sundry. But it is possible for a note to go out with the wedding invitation asking those who wish to receive Holy Communion with the bride and bridegroom to indicate the same in their reply. At the service it can then be made plain that only those who have signified their intention to do so are expected to communicate.

The rubric in the 1928 Service says that after the Gospel "the Priest shall then continue the Order of Holy Communion, the new-married persons remaining before the Holy Table until the end of the Service". If this is done, after the bride and bridegroom have received, the other communicants come up in succession and kneel on either side of them, and there is a great sense of fellowship. In administering to the bride and bridegroom it is appropriate to say the words to both of them together, and indeed to divide a single piece of bread (or wafer) between them.

The 1966 Alternative Form is clear that the Communion comes after the prayer for child-bearing (or the preceding Collect if that be not said), but does not direct that the third of the Marriage prayers and blessing should be said before the final Communion blessing, "The peace of God, etc". This was ordered in 1928, and it is a pity that this very beautiful prayer should be omitted, even though the Collect provided for the Communion is a prayer for the gift of love. If, as is permitted, the Collect, Epistle, and Gospel of the day were substituted, it would be possible then that this important element in the prayers would be left out entirely.

THE END OF THE SERVICE

When there is no Communion, the address being ended, there will probably be the second hymn, and then the dismissal of the congregation (Alternative Service). It is good to indicate, perhaps by moving away from the position immediately in front of the couple, that the Marriage Service proper is now ended. The prayer and blessing which follow concern the congregation, not the bride and bridegroom. Some such words as these may be a help. "The service is over. Let us spend a few moments in silent prayer commending John and Mary to God's care as they set out on their new life together. (Pause.) And now a prayer for ourselves." There follows the second of the Table prayers and the blessing.

We shall have told the couple that when they see the priest rise from his knees they should do the same, and the organ will begin to play. The best man should have been instructed to escort bridesmaids and parents into the vestry where they greet the happy pair before the signing of the registers. It is important that the minister supervise the signing with care, and remind the bride to sign her maiden name. If too many people sign as witnesses, it will make the books untidy, and it is well if they are content to have the required minimum of two and no more. All names have to be copied for the quarterly returns, so if any signatures are illegible (and they often are), it is essential to make a note of what they are meant to signify. The Marriage Certificate is a copy of the entry in the Registers, and if all the signatories sign the certificate as well as the registers, it is not only a copy, but also a more "live" reminder of the original.

The atmosphere in the vestry varies enormously from one wedding to another, from a solemn religious silence where no one dares to speak above a whisper to an orgy of embracing and hilarity. We should aim at something between the two. Churches differ in their rule about photography in the vestry. It would appear innocuous enough, but the photo of the signing should be posed after the actual signing has been done. It remains only to give the bride her marriage lines, line up the procession, signal to the organist that all is ready for the Mendelssohn March, or whatever music they have chosen instead, and send them down the church to face their smiling friends and a battery of cameras outside.

The utmost care should be exercised in seeing that the registers are correctly filled in and signed, and reference should be made to *Suggestions for the Guidance of the Clergy with reference to the Marriage and Registration Acts, etc.*, which is issued by the Registrar General.

15

The Follow-up

The follow-up of a wedding begins immediately after the
newly married couple have walked down the church. While
the photographs are being taken there is an opportunity to
speak to some of the guests. We, like them, are friends of
the bride and bridegroom, and not merely officials doing a
job. We share in the general rejoicing. Some clergymen are
naturally gifted in outgoing friendliness to all and sundry,
and assume the leading part in the good-natured banter of
the occasion. If this can be done without loss of dignity, well
and good. Others express their friendliness in quieter ways,
and they need not be downcast because they cannot emulate
their more boisterous brethren. We are all made differently,
and it is sincerity that counts most.

If the minister is asked to be in one of the photographs,
either robed or in his cassock, he should of course comply.
Some go further than this and actually propose themselves
to be taken with the bride and bridegroom. The idea is that
they should have a reminder of the priest who officiated. I
should myself be chary of making the suggestion, for it seems
better manners to wait till one is asked. The same applies to
attendance at the reception. If invited, we should accept but
not take an invitation for granted. In small parishes where
there will not be more than half a dozen weddings in the
year the clergyman and his wife will almost certainly be invited in the ordinary way. In such a case the usual courtesy
of a present will be given, but it will be understood that it
can be something quite small and inexpensive. In parishes

where there is a large number of weddings probably only those couples who are closely associated with the church will invite the priest. It would be impossible, in terms of time alone, for him to go to them all. In some cases where he has not received a formal invitation he may be asked verbally in the vestry if he can "drop in" at the reception. This he should do, if only for a few minutes, if other engagements permit. Every occasion which brings us in contact with people, however remote it may seem from the preaching of the gospel, can be to the glory of God. Jesus did not preach at the wedding feast, but his presence made it a happier occasion than it would otherwise have been, and what happened there "led his disciples to believe in him" (N.E.B.).

If the couple are going to live in the parish, then a visit to them soon after their return from their honeymoon is a good thing. The main object will be friendliness, but it should be natural to have a prayer before leaving, asking God's blessing on the new home. For those who would like a simple service of Blessing of the House, there is one issued by the S.P.C.K. If a single prayer is all that is appropriate, then "Visit, we beseech thee, O Lord, this place (house, dwelling) . . ." from the Order of Compline may suffice. But many priests will prefer to use extempore prayer, with the Lord's Prayer and the Grace. When they are going to live elsewhere, as is so often the case, the couple should be commended to their new parish priest.

The link with the parish church in which they are married is not severed completely even though a couple moves away. For one thing there will very likely be occasional visits at week-ends to the girl's parents, and at such times we can make contact again. For family reasons as well as for sentiment they may want to bring their first baby back to be christened. In this case we have to explain carefully that it can only be with the knowledge and support of their parish priest. Particular care is needed if the baptismal discipline of the two parishes concerned is not the same.

For those who have moved away as well as for those who remain in the parish a letter from the vicar on the anniversary of the wedding is an important part of the follow-up. Each letter should be different, though there is bound to be a general similarity. A little care in keeping records will help us to refer to some particular event at the wedding—a hymn chosen, or the subject of the address—and any item of parish news likely to be of interest can be included. Such letters are nearly always answered, and bring news of the couple, important items of which can be entered on the card index. These annual letters can be kept up year after year, though in parishes of any size the work may call for secretarial help.

Another plan which is being increasingly worked in some parishes is an annual Marriage Thanksgiving Service, usually on a Sunday evening. All those married in the church are specially invited, though those married elsewhere, and the general congregation, are equally made welcome. There is no need to depart from the Order for Evening Prayer, with appropriate hymns and sermon, but a place can be made for special thanksgiving and for the renewing of marriage vows. If couples are asked to stand and renew their promises, obviously the clergyman and his wife should not be exempt! I am bound to say that I have never myself tried this type of service on a Sunday evening, but have been told of the great impression made, not least by the vicar and his wife joining with all the others in the act of rededication.

Another variation of this general idea, which I have found to be much appreciated, is a wedding reunion at which only the invited couples are present. Let us say that the reunion is to be of all those married in the parish church in the last five years and that this involves a hundred and fifty couples. Properly printed invitations are sent out in the name of the vicar and his wife to a Reunion of those married in St Peter's, on a Saturday at 7.30 p.m. in the church, followed by a reception at 8 o'clock in the Hall, and R.S.V.P. is put at the bottom. A few—very few—will not bother to reply. Of the rest, some are too far away to come, some cannot leave the baby, some have previous engagements, or invent an excuse. But a good number will reply that they accept with gratitude.

The service should be kept to about twenty-five minutes and include the most popular wedding hymns, the reading of a lesson (perhaps 1 Cor. 13 in the N.E.B.), a very short address, and prayers which include some form of rededication. The playing of Mendelssohn's Wedding March is an obvious finale.

The reception should be as well done as the resources of the parish can afford. The vicar and his wife receive the guests. As they are not all known to each other they might be asked to wear name tabs—an excellent aid to the memory of the vicar. Refreshments are served by some parish group (it *could* be the Youth Fellowship and not necessarily the Mothers' Union) and a genuine wedding cake is an essential part. There need not be any speeches, but a short first-class programme of entertainment, with the vicar bringing the evening to a close with a few words of wisdom before the final prayer. The cost of such an evening should be borne by the P.C.C. who must learn to see the care of those married in the church as a piece of important pastoral work.

16

Problem Cases

We ought not to think of problem people, only of people with problems. There is nobody without problems altogether, but some seem to have the kind which are very difficult to solve. It is the same with the couples we prepare for marriage. They all have problems, and it is our heaven-sent task to help them towards a solution. But there are a certain number who come within well-defined categories that present special difficulties. Though we discuss them under the general heading of problem cases, we shall not forget that each is a couple of infinite worth to God, and that we are to help them as much as we can to normal fulfilment.

1. THE IMMATURE

This is very much a matter of degree and there are few people who do not suffer from immaturity of one kind or another. Those who pride themselves on what they would call an adult attitude to sex may actually be emotionally far from maturity, and spiritually naïve in the extreme. And every couple we see needs to grow in self-knowledge and knowledge of one another, and of life in general, before they can be said to have reached maturity. Nevertheless there are some who show in unmistakable ways that they are immature beyond the average. It is not just a matter of age, though it stands to reason that the younger a couple is in years the more likely they are to suffer from some deficiency of emotional make-up which will make their marriage unsatisfactory.

There are those who are frightened by the idea of sexual intercourse. For one or more of a variety of reasons they may think it wicked, or at least vulgar. This can be the result of faulty teaching, or unpleasant experiences in childhood. It may even be due to a false view of the Christian stand-point in spite of all that the New Testament says about the rightness of the physical relationship. There are cases of this type of immaturity which need treatment by a psychiatrist, and we should not hesitate to recommend this, even to insist on it with all the powers we have, short of absolute compulsion. For to allow a couple to get married when there is no normal delight in the sex factor, but only fear and scruple, is asking for trouble.

In many cases, however, the need is not for professional psychiatric treatment, but for the reassurance which we can give as Christian pastors. We must stress the divine nature of the gift of sex, its beauty and purity (to use an unfashionable word) within marriage. We should take special care to see that such a couple has read a book which deals fully and frankly with the physical side of marriage, and if possible has attended one of the M.G.C. courses. At the same time we should warn them that everything does not always go according to plan, and that there is nothing to worry about in this. Even if it takes weeks, or sometimes months, most marriages are capable of reaching a thoroughly satisfactory adjustment. Fear of failure need not be entertained.

Reluctance to accept the idea of intercourse is by no means the only mark of immaturity. There can be an over-emphasis on the physical, so that marriage is thought of only as sleeping together, to the exclusion of every other aspect. Babies, and a life of companionship, do not enter into the picture at all. To say that this is a special danger with the very young is not to deny that there are some couples in their teens who make successful marriages. But we must face the fact that the very young are more likely than others to be swept off their feet by passion alone, and to embark on

a marriage which has insufficient basis to be permanent.
Here we may find an immaturity of character, very likely
an unusually low standard of education, and almost certainly a complete absence of any Christian conviction.

Ought we in such a case to try to get the couple to delay
the marriage? Realism compels us to say that the chances
are not very great. If the parents are in agreement, it may
be possible; but then we have to face the probability that
the couple will sleep together without waiting to be married, and one day a marriage will be arranged in a hurry so
as to give legitimate status to a baby that is to be born. It
may be best to show by the extra care we take in the preparation that we have reason for concern in the particular
case, and to follow up after the marriage. If we have gained
their confidence during the time of preparation, it should
be possible to arrange a further interview after the honeymoon. Above all, we should try to draw such couples into
the fellowship of the church, without which no one is completely mature.

Whatever the cause of immaturity, or the particular symp-
toms of it, we have to try to help the couple to grow, and
only in rare cases shall we be right to try to stop a wedding
taking place. Paul E. Johnson, in his book *Pastoral Ministration*, has this to say:

> Most young people are immature when they agree to marry,
> and marriage may be just the experience to mature them.
> Even as counsellors may seek to appraise readiness for mar-
> riage, they are not omniscient as to future developments; and
> after all it is the right of the young people to decide whether
> they will marry.[1]

2. PREGNANCY BEFORE MARRIAGE

It is common knowledge that a certain number of those who
come to get married are already expecting a baby. Far more

[1] James Nisbet, 1955. The section on Pre-marital Counselling is a
valuable part of this most useful book.

have undoubtedly had intercourse together but have taken the precautions necessary to avoid a pregnancy. It is not very often that the fact of pre-marital intercourse is admitted; but if a child is on the way, it is much more likely to be. In one way or another, by the haste with which arrangements are being made or the embarrassment of the couple at the interview, it becomes evident. They are probably wanting to tell us, and we should make it easy for them to do so, without of course making the suggestion that we had jumped to that conclusion already.

There is often a real sense of sorrow, even of remorse, at what has happened. We have to ask ourselves whether the shame is for the pregnancy or for the intercourse which caused it. Is it the stigma of having a baby before the time that is chiefly worrying them, or is there really a sign of penitence for the wrong done? Any small experience in dealing with conscience, our own as well as other people's, teaches us how difficult it is to discern motive. Under wise tuition what may be little more than sorrow for being found out, and consequent loss of face, may be deepened into a genuine penitence.

Perhaps the first thing that needs to be said is that the sin does not consist in having a baby but in the anticipation of marriage which went before. Many couples who have avoided a pregnancy have nevertheless sinned in exactly the same way. Not that it makes sin less sinful to know that others are sinners too, but we do want to be sure that if they have feelings of guilt, they know what it is of which they are guilty. Sometimes when this is put to them a couple may begin to feel less guilty after all!

Not for a moment should we wish to condone sin. But the habit of mind which has persisted in making sexual sins more heinous than any other is entirely out of harmony with the New Testament. Among the seven deadly sins enumerated by the theologians, lust takes its place alongside pride, covetousness, envy, and the rest, neither worse nor better. And among sexual sins there are surely degrees of guilt. There is a world of difference between a *roué* who has lived promiscuously and a young man who has always been faithful to the girl he loves, but in a moment of passion has been swept off his feet, and perhaps been desperately sorry about it afterwards. Not all cases are as easy to distinguish as that, but in every instance we need to remember that we serve God who sent the Son into the world, not to condemn the world but that the world might be saved through him.

Our duty is to take people where we find them and try to lead them to newness of life. In the case of a pregnant woman this may sometimes mean doing all we can to stop the marriage. It may happen that the father of the child had no intention of marriage until faced with the fact of the pregnancy. The couple may not be in love at all, and may be in every way quite unsuited to each other. For them to get married simply to make the birth legitimate is quite irresponsible. By some miracle it could happen that they would come to love each other and so create a home for the child, and subsequent children, to be brought up in. But the risk is very great. It is surely better for the child to be born illegitimate and adopted into a good home, and for the mother and father to be helped individually to a new life.

But in many cases there was already intention to marry, and the pregnancy is the result of unwise anticipation. Indeed the length to which "petting" seems to be permitted during engagement, or even before, makes it a matter of wonder that there are so many—and there still are—who come to their wedding day as virgins. Young people of high principles and Christian convictions are influenced by the general trend, and will sometimes go as far as it is possible to go in love making, only stopping short of actual intercourse. Quite apart from the moral aspect, the strain that is put upon two virile young people is well-nigh intolerable. We need to start far back in our teaching and inculcate an attitude of restraint in the earlier stages. Otherwise more and more people will go the whole way, and lose so much in the process.

Yet when we have before us a couple who are expecting a baby, we shall not be condemning. We shall speak to them of the need of forgiveness of *all sin*, of which this is only one. And we shall urge them to forget the things of the past and reach out to what lies ahead. There is no reason why they should not grow into responsible parents and builders of a real home, even though they have acted irresponsibly. We shall of course help them to have as normal a wedding as possible. A shocking old wives' tale is that a woman already pregnant may not be married in church and there are some who still believe it. Whether the bride wears a white dress is a matter for her to decide. If it is intended as a symbol of virginity, she is technically unable to do so, but God who reads the heart may see that there are others who get away with a white wedding who are far less qualified to do so. Neighbours can gossip and condemn, but with the story of John 8.1–11 in mind we should take our stand, not with the scribes and Pharisees, but with the Saviour.

3. THE UNSURE

Under this heading we are thinking, not so much of those who through immaturity are in danger of making a wrong choice, but of people of sound character who are beset by doubts almost at the last minute. This trouble is much more common than is generally admitted, and attacks particularly those who are slightly older, who are above average intelligence, and who care most about their Christian integrity. Like Cassius, they think too much, though they do not always have a lean and hungry look, and are not dangerous except to themselves.

As the time of the wedding approaches, a serious-minded couple naturally senses the mounting tension. They know that the step they are to take is irrevocable, and the knowledge of this can be enough to cause grave doubts. Add to this the strain of waiting for marriage, particularly in those who have kept their sights high. All this can drive away temporarily any emotional feeling of love. Now there *may* be cases where the absence of love is revealed at the last minute as a warning to break it off. But in the cases we are thinking of the couple have chosen each other in calmer moments, have known love and companionship; and if they are devout Christians, are conscious of God's guidance in their lives which has brought them to this point. It would be sheer madness to reverse it all on the ground of last-minute "nerves" which can be explained on perfectly natural grounds. Therefore we have got to reassure in every way we can those who are plagued with such doubts.

Doubts could also arise through a feeling of guilt. We must discern between over-anxiety, scrupulosity or over-conscientiousness, and genuine conviction of wrong-doing. The one must be dealt with along the lines suggested above, the other by helping the person to confess the sin and receive forgiveness. The question will arise as to whether confession should be made to the partner to be. The guidance of the priest will probably be needed here. I believe myself that there should be the utmost frankness. Engaged couples like to tell each other all about their past lives. This will include former friendships, whether serious or not. There need be no suggestion of "confession" about this: most people have been more or less in love with someone else before they found the right one. It is nothing to be ashamed of.

But what if there has been an *affaire*? I believe that, even though it has been repented of and forgiven by God, it should be disclosed before marriage. Sexual intercourse changes the status both of a man and of a woman. Virginity is a priceless gift to bring to marriage. There was a time when it was expected of the woman but not necessarily of the man. The equality of the sexes is restored today in our neo-pagan society by expecting it of neither. The Christian standard is to expect it of both. And where this is not the case there should be confession of it, and forgiveness. I recall an instance of a man who, for his own peace of mind if for nothing else, knew that he had to tell his future wife of an aberration years before. It was a single act, and many would have dismissed it as a peccadillo. The telling of it caused distress, but nothing like the distress which would have been if it had been uncovered after the marriage, when the sense of having been deceived would have been added.[1] Doubts of this kind do often need our help for their resolving.

Whether or not they can be put into a category of special problem cases, almost all who come to us are people with problems. We are available to help them, not as those who know all the answers, still less as people without any problems of our own, but as fellow-humans who have begun to discover the richness of life in Christ. Through all our preparation talks, even on the apparently most unrelated topics, we are inviting them to join us in this wonderful discovery. We shall not always get them very far, though we shall hope to be able to follow up the work begun at the time of their marriage, and we should implore them to come back to us in case of any difficulty. Now and again we shall have the great joy of seeing the fruit of our labours. If the Christian Faith is going to revive in the *homes* of our land—as it well may—we shall be contributing much towards it as we give the best we have to the work of Marriage Preparation.

[1] This actual case can be quoted because there is no possibility of anyone being able to identify the couple. The greatest care is needed never to betray confidences.

Bibliography

There is a large literature on the subject of friendship, love, and marriage, from which the following is a useful selection.

FOR RECOMMENDING TO ENGAGED COUPLES

The Threshold of Marriage, Church Information Office.
A booklet of 32 pages, probably the best value for giving away. It deals adequately with most aspects of marriage, but further reading is advisable in the majority of cases.

Guide to Marriage, by Leslie J. Tizard, Allen and Unwin.
Probably the best book for those who want the sex aspect fully, yet simply, dealt with. Also gives wise advice on other subjects, from in-laws to hire purchase. The style is popular and light, with flashes of humour. The approach is thoroughly Christian.

The Sex Factor in Marriage, by Helena Wright, Benn.
Written by a doctor, it is exactly what the title suggests. It could be preferable to Tizard for any who are too sophisticated to enjoy the "raciness" of the latter.

The Art of Marriage, by Mary Macauley, Penguin.
Another excellent manual, covering the same ground as Wright. Also written by a doctor with real understanding.

Background to Marriage, by Anne Proctor, Longmans, Green.
Not a textbook on sex, but a deeply Christian discussion of the spiritual values of every aspect of marriage. Many married couples ought to read it, but it is invaluable also for those about to be married who are prepared to think deeply. Thoroughly readable.

Your Marriage, by Martin Parsons, Hodder and Stoughton.
Basically a commentary on the Marriage Service, it is an expansion of the kind of things which any priest will want to say to those he prepares.

Passion and Marriage, by Constance Robinson, S.P.C.K.
For the more thoughtful couple this should be compulsory reading. Recommended also for general use. Outstanding as a Christian contribution to the subject of sex.

FOR MORE GENERAL PREPARATION

Sex and Sanity, by Stuart Barton Babbage, Hodder and Stoughton.
A useful little book putting the Christian approach positively and with reasonableness.

A Christian's Guide to Love, Sex and Marriage, by A. Morgan Derham, Hodder and Stoughton.
Well worth circulating in the youth club.

Morality—Old and New, by E. Parkinson Smith and A. Graham Ikin, Peter Smith.
A sensible discussion on some of the moral problems.

Loving, by David Sheppard, Scripture Union.
One of a series of booklets described as a publishing venture for teenagers who do not normally read books. An outstanding production.

FOR THE PRIEST'S OWN READING

All those already mentioned will be helpful to anyone engaged in preparing couples for marriage. The following will also be found specially useful.

A Handbook to Marriage and Marriage Guidance, by Theodor Bovet, Longmans, Green.
"The extraordinary breadth of his thought, combining as it does the approaches of medicine, of psychology, of philosophy, and of theology, entitles him to be heard with attention and with respect" (David Mace in the Foreword).

Men and Women, by Gilbert Russell, S.C.M. Press.
A basic study, not about sex but about men and women.

Learning to Love, by Alan H. B. Ingleby, Robert Hale.
A book for parents, with much that is of value to any parish priest who tries to help young people.

Pastoral Ministration, by Paul E. Johnson, James Nisbet.
The section on Marriage Counselling is not the least important part of this invaluable book.

A List of Useful Addresses

National Marriage Guidance Council
58 Queen Anne Street, London W.1.
There are many local Marriage Guidance Councils, the addresses of which can be supplied by the above, but normally they will be found in the telephone directory.

The Family Planning Association
64 Sloane Street, London S.W.1.
Local branches exist all over the country. The priest should know the addresses of clinics in his neighbourhood so as to be able to commend couples needing advice on contraception. The Association is not *only* concerned with birth control but also runs sub-fertility clinics.

The Church of England Board for Social Responsibility
Department of Moral and Social Welfare
Church House, Dean's Yard, Westminster S.W.1.
There is often a Moral Welfare Worker attached to a Deanery, and most Dioceses have a Moral Welfare Association. Addresses will be found in the Diocesan Year Book.

The Mothers' Union, Mary Sumner House
Tufton Street, Westminster S.W.1.

The Church of England Men's Society
Fulham Palace, London S.W.6.

The Bible Reading Fellowship
148 Buckingham Palace Road, London S.W.1.

The Scripture Union, 5 Wigmore Street, London W.1.

The Society for Promoting Christian Knowledge
Holy Trinity Church, Marylebone Road, London N.W.1.

The Registrar of the Court of Faculties
1 The Sanctuary, Westminster S.W.1.

The Registrar General, Somerset House, Strand, London W.C.2.

The Church Pastoral-Aid Society
Falcon Court, 32 Fleet Street, London E.C.4.

Index